Light and Silence

Growing Up in My Mother's Alaska

Janet Brown

Light and Silence
Growing Up in My Mother's Alaska
By Janet Brown

Copyright©2015 ThingsAsian Press

Photographs from the author's private collection.

ThingsAsian Press
San Francisco, California. USA
www.thingsasianpress.com

Printed in Hong Kong

ISBN-10: 1-934159-56-5
ISBN-13: 978-1-934159-56-9

Contents

For my little brother, Robert John (1956-1980)

Two years before she left for Alaska, 1948

Introduction

She was a Catholic school girl who planned to major in Latin just because she loved the language, but World War II intervened. Her younger brothers joined the Marines the minute they were old enough. She contributed to the war effort by taking a job as a ticket clerk at Pennsylvania Station instead of going on to college.

He was a Coast Guard veteran who had just returned from post-war Italy with a fistful of campaign medals and some memories he refused to talk about, a boy who had left high school in his second year to work in his father's bakery. 'The depression hit and the old man thought that going on relief was a disgrace," he said much later.

She was a New Yorker to the core. He was from Pennsylvania Dutch country. If not for her ticket clerk job, they would never have met. Their first date was a walk through Central Park in the snow. He caught a cold that knocked him flat; she came to his apartment with hot soup.

She was the American Girl of every soldier's dream: well-scrubbed, long-legged, virginal, with a dazzling smile. He was short with more than a dash of Bogart and a grin that any politician would kill for. He had nothing and she had a dream that was as unshakable as it was impractical. They married.

She had suitors before she met him, but they all had solid visions for the future, none of which corresponded to her own. "I married your father because I knew he would take me to Alaska," she told me.

They set up their household in a tenement apartment on Manhattan's Upper East Side, covering the bathtub in the kitchen with a wooden door to turn it into a table and splatter-painting the ancient wooden floor with confetti flecks of bright color. They had heavy, Roman-striped draperies custom made to cover the ugly views from their windows. They built bookshelves and bought a martini pitcher, a phonograph, and black plastic 78 rpm records encased in thick, cream-colored paper albums.

They both loved to read, although he was dismayed to discover that she had packed a copy of Daphne DuMaurier's *Rebecca* when they went on their honeymoon camping trip to Cape Hatteras. They went to the ballet, the opera, the symphony, and the theater when they could scrounge cheap tickets. They haunted the Metropolitan Museum of Art, the Cloisters, and the city's multitude of public libraries.

She didn't work once they were married, From the very beginning she hated to keep house and reluctantly learned to cook. She wanted to be a writer. He wanted a family. "You," she told me, "were my present to your father."

They scrimped, with style and eagerness, knowing that being poor in Manhattan was only a temporary state for them. They bought an army surplus jeep and a small trailer, into which they packed everything they owned. They drove out of New York City toward Canada, with me, still a baby, sitting in my mother's lap. They camped from the East Coast, through Canada, and into Alaska.

Not yet a state, Alaska was wide open and empty. The federal government had dusted off the Homestead Act in hopes of attracting young settlers who were willing to raise families in the wilderness. Small 10-acre homesite tracts and homestead sites of 160 acres were available to anyone who had enough money to pay the filing fee.

She wanted to go into the far north. He pointed out the practicalities of living in the mild coastal climate of Southcentral Alaska. They found a clearing near a lake, surrounded by dark spruce trees, and built a tiny two-room cabin.

Within three years, a random accident, the brushing of a co-worker's cap brim against my father's eyeball, would lead to a detached retina and impaired vision. My mother, with two small children and pregnant with her third, fought to remain in Alaska. They stayed, and paid for that decision, over and over again.

The life my mother lived was difficult, but it was her own. She chose it, she shaped it, and she savored it. This is her story.

My mother had grown up in a privileged East Coast bubble. a Manhattan girl who was taken on summer trips to Maine where her mother's family had lived in Castine for 300 years. The Wescotts lost their money and much of their land during the Depression, but the saltbox family house was still theirs, full of treasures brought home from clipper ship voyages, and history enshrined in carefully tended photograph albums and journals.

Her father's family had a similar enclave on Long Island, but without the aristocratic undertones. The Meehans were Irish who had become successful in a couple of generations, but my grandfather, a well-to-do attorney, had to fight hard to win my grandmother. Her family well remembered the signs that told jobseekers "No Irish need apply."

My mother grew up with stories of the day nobody could find her when she was very small until the cook discovered her asleep on the bottom tier of the tea wagon. One of her first memories was the sharp smell of fresh ink that pervaded her father's library when he first opened a newly delivered book by cutting its pages open with a special paper knife. The Depression changed her life of course, but even then the comfort she lived in was enviable.

She was a good Catholic girl, clad in a navy blue and white uniform five days a week, going to a school that lay in the shadow of St. Patrick's Cathedral. She made good grades, she was an obedient daughter, but in her heart she had an unspoken plan. She would someday leave Manhattan and live in Alaska.

This had been her dream since she was seven years old. Her father gave her a copy of *The Snow Baby*, the story of Admiral Robert Peary's daughter, Marie, who was born in Greenland and spent years as a child living with Inuit people in the Arctic. It caught her imagination and she became obsessed with the idea of living in America's Arctic—Alaska.

When World War II began to consume the lives of both soldiers and civilians, hurtling women into the workforce to replace the men who had gone to fight, my mother found out that Elmendorf Air Force Base in Anchorage, Alaska, needed women to staff their offices. She wanted to go, she prepared a letter of application, but when she showed it to her mother, that idea died. My grandmother forbade it and that should have been the end of the matter. It wasn't.

After my mother's brothers joined the Marines, my mother began to meet their friends. All of the young men who surrounded her were Irish Catholic boys from New York, or New Englanders whose heritage almost matched her own. She came close to falling in love a couple of times but "they wouldn't take me to Alaska," she explained to me years later. My father did, and my grandmother never forgave him for it.

My father was the son of a Pennsylvania Dutch girl whose family came to America before the Revolution, found the soft and fertile farmland of the Lehigh Valley, and never left. His father left Germany when he was thirteen, traveling by ship with his older brothers to another country where he eventually became a businessman and property owner. My father's life was solidly bourgeois until the Depression came. Then the war took him out of Pennsylvania and he never went back.

World War II gave my father a perspective and knowledge that my mother hadn't yet acquired. When they reached Alaska, he adapted quickly; my mother didn't. Her dream had been the pristine sweep of Arctic snow and the roseate picture of a small girl's early childhood. She expected Eskimos and malemutes and the squeak of dry snow under fur-booted feet. She doubtless was looking forward to witnessing her first seal hunt. What she got instead was a small cabin in a place with a climate that was usually wet, cloudy, and sullen. Instead of perfect isolation where she could form her own society of books and music, passing her manners and values to her children without interference, she found herself in a community of no more than one hundred people, all white, all rural, all very West Coast. Up to that point in her life, my mother had never met anyone from the West Coast.

This wasn't her dream and the force of that hit her hard. It took her years to understand the virtues of her new place in the world and the people who inhabited it with her. There were few women in the nearby town of Anchor Point, and they almost were all from small towns and farms in the Pacific Northwest. They entertained themselves with square dances, potluck suppers, pie socials. My New York-bred mother went into a severe form of culture shock. She kept to herself for a long time before she finally began to make friends.

I really think she had believed that Alaska would be a world that was perhaps separated from books, ballet, art, and opera but still cared deeply about these things. She never intended to abandon her upbringing. She planned to pass her manners, her values, and her history on to her children, but within a setting that was wild, beautiful, and untouched. When her little girls began to speak in flat Oregonian accents, this threw her into fits of rage.

"You little bugger," women would say to us affectionately, or "Bless your little heart." My mother would sit quietly while trying not to wince; she sternly stamped out any tendency we might have had to repeat these phrases.

Her Alaska wasn't what she had envisioned and her children became Alaskans in a way she never imagined. On the rare occasions that she took us back to the East Coast, we never really belonged there, which shocked her. We were supposed to be good New York girls, even though we were brought up almost on another continent, in a place that was another world.

I started to write about my mother to keep her alive as she began to dwindle. As I wrote, I began to understand, in a way that I never had before, the woman who had given birth to me, and was struck to the heart by how young she was when I first knew her. Her life astounded me. I don't think I could have ever survived the existence she had chosen for herself—

at least not with her deep-rooted sense of joy and commitment.

I ended my version of my mother's story at the time when she turned forty, because that was when she began the long process of constructing a new and very different life for herself. It was also the time of my childhood's end, and the beginning of drastic changes that would transform the Alaska that I had grown up in.

There is a whole subculture of Homestead Kids, those of us who were shaped in mid-20th century Alaska by a way of life that was locked in the 1800s. When times of crisis struck, our parents still sent and received telegrams. Dowsers, or "water-witchers," wandered through our yards with cleft willow branches, waiting for that spasmodic downward jerk to point out the spot where a well could be successfully excavated. Our fathers butchered freshly killed, illegally hunted moose on the kitchen table; our mothers dug potatoes with their bare hands from gardens that would be frozen rock-solid by the next day. Mail-order catalogs were our shopping malls, and many of us went to one-room schoolhouses where all eight grades of a grammar school were instructed at the same time. We wore hand-me-down clothing without shame, and thought store-bought sliced white bread was a delicacy. When we finally encountered modern life, our culture shock was as immense as the delight we felt at no longer having to haul wood and water, or use an outhouse.

My own children spent the first part of their childhoods in Alaska, but not in the way I had. They grew up with electricity, running water, color television, refrigerators, and fresh fruit that was available even in winter. They went to bookstores, movie theaters, swimming pools, and roller rinks. They walked on sidewalks and rode their bicycles on bike paths. Their Alaska was a universe away from the one I had known as a child.

This book is for them, but I also hope that Homestead Kids of my generation may read it, laugh a little, shudder occasionally, and remember. My mother, their mothers, gave us a time and place to grow up in that is gone for good—unless we tell the stories.

Although I will never again live in Alaska, there are times when I miss the legacy that my mother gave me. She placed me in a landscape that had no room for lies or pretentions, where possessions weren't the measure of a person's worth. She taught me to be at ease with silence and limitless space, to savor the sharp, clear scent of wild berries just before they are killed by frost, and the smell of heat rising from sunlit earth. She made me understand that there is no such thing as bad weather on a beach, and that there are few troubles that can't be diminished by spending time outdoors under a sky filled with clear and dazzling stars. She gave me the ability to live with very little and showed me how to be happy with what I had, just so long as there was something to read close at hand. Most of all, she instilled in me a refusal to live a confined life, one that is smothered by conventions and ordinary dreams. She made the decision to live in Alaska when she was a little girl, and her choice has enriched my life in ways that I still continue to discover as I begin to age.

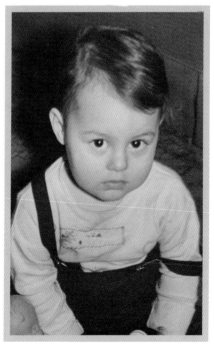

Me as a newly arrived Alaskan, 1950

My mother and me near our lake, 1951

Light and Silence

Part One
What She Wanted

Chapter One

Shortly before Christmas, after the tree went up but before the gifts were given and the feast was put on the table, at a time of year that she had always loved, my mother left her home and never went back.

Age first took her balance, then her appetite, then her ability to walk. When a woman can no longer make her way to the bathroom alone, she faces hard and painful choices. My mother was luckier than many other old women. The daughter who always loved her best found a tree-encircled, quiet house owned by a woman who took care of elderly people and who immediately liked our mother.

Four years earlier, I saw her teeter and fall. It was an omen that was as threatening as breaking a hip. Gradually, but not slowly, her balance deteriorated, and with it went her confidence and her independence.

My mother would probably have claimed that her independence began to wither when she realized she could no longer drive. For decades she had been used to hopping into her car at will and taking off on tiny adventures—going to the movies or to buy groceries. The distance she traveled was unimportant; it was the choice that mattered, and the spontaneity. When she gave up her driver's license, her world began to shrink and "I wish I could still drive," was a keynote of her conversations over the following years.

My mother had always been a woman with a drive-by life. She loved fleeting encounters with random people, anecdotes that concluded when she hopped into her car and drove away. She was nourished by these meetings and when she no longer could go out to find them, I think she began to starve a little. Slowly she began to shut down.

She lived close to the Arctic Circle, in Fairbanks, a small town on the banks of the Tanana River. She had a lovely little apartment that I coveted—an open room with large windows overlooking the river, and a dark, cozy, book-filled bedroom. It was compact and "just right," like Goldilocks' porridge. There was room for everything my mother loved to do—cooking, reading, listening to music, and watching movies. But it was out in the country. The bus that took aging people into town didn't come as far as my mother's house, and taxis put a whopping hole in her budget. To go anywhere, she had to be driven by her family.

She was surrounded by an enclave of family. My sister's husband had built her apartment specifically for her and she needed to take only two steps through a covered garage to reach the back door of my sister's house. Her son-in-law's parents lived directly across from her apartment, and his siblings had two other households within walking distance. At first there was a wide pool of transportation possibilities for my mother; eventually there was only my sister and her husband.

My mother went to Weight Watchers and to Curves, to my sister's Toastmaster meetings, to the library—but it wasn't the same for her. These outings weren't spontaneous; they were on someone else's schedule. For her, much of the fun was fading from her excursions, even though they were no different from what she would have done had she made them on her own.

When I was little, I would go out to our old Chevrolet sedan, sit in it, and pretend to drive. I had noticed the sense of joy and freedom that my mother found behind the steering wheel and I wanted that for myself.

My mother learned to drive when she was pregnant with her fourth child; for years she went nowhere without a cluster of children in the back seat of her Chevy. But she was in another world when she drove her car. It was a socially sanctioned way to escape the housekeeping she detested and the cooking that consumed her life—the inexorable three meals a day for five children and a husband. There were no demands of her when she drove; her children knew better than to interrupt her concentration upon the road. Her happiness was palpable, and that was what I tried to capture as I imagined that control of the car was mine.

As soon as she could, once I was old enough to be left in charge of my brother and sisters, my mother made her escape even more private. She would put on a fresh coat of red lipstick, blot it by kissing us all goodbye, get in her car and drive off to pick up the mail and buy groceries. It was a trip that took several hours, all of them hers. She'd return with stories of who she saw, what they chatted about. Her car was her sanctuary and her lifeline. My mother took to driving the way other women took to drink.

And now that was gone. She did her best to substitute the telephone, using it for long visits with her daughters, her nephew in Manhattan, her cousin in Florida. She became the conduit of information between all of us, but that lacked the savor of finding her own stories. Then her hearing began to fade.

My mother had a bulging bank account of stories from her eighty-plus years of life and she had always dreamed of being a writer. As her life became more contained, this would have been the time for her to put her stories on paper, but she didn't do it. For her, the pleasure was in the attention, immediate and gratifying, that she received when she told anecdotes out loud. A storyteller in the oral tradition, she should have followed my sister into Toastmasters. She would have been a star.

Now she was in a house where she wasn't the only old person. There were four other people who were cared for in the same place. Some were older than she was, some had more pronounced limitations of age. All of them valued their privacy and their dignity as much as my mother did. She was part of a small community again, no longer dependent upon her children for phone calls, conversation, excursions. When my sister found this new home for my mother, she gave her a new source of stories. "We tell ourselves stories in order to live," Joan Didion said and I hoped that was true. I wanted with all my heart for my mother to begin to find fresh stories.

Part One
What She Wanted

Our homestead road in the hills

Thanksgiving 1952

Light and Silence

Chapter Two

My mother never learned to swim or ride a bicycle. She probably would never have learned to drive, if my father hadn't lost his eyesight. I don't swim, drive, or ride a bicycle; I am, as a friend recently pointed out, my mother's daughter in many ways. Because he is a friend, he pointed out the good things I have in common with my mother. There are other shared qualities that I have spent time trying to uproot and still others that are embedded so deep that it would take years of therapy and several cases of dynamite to dislodge them.

I never wanted to be like my mother, even when I most loved her. Physically we were so dissimilar that until I was shown a picture of my grandmother as a child and saw the resemblance between her face and mine, I was positive I was adopted. My mother was taller than most of the women we knew, black Irish, with fair skin, hazel eyes, and hair that was far beyond dark brown. Against her skin, it looked like ebony to me, just like Snow White's. I was olive-skinned, brown-eyed—a dark little gypsy. When my grandmother first saw me, her reaction was "She looks just like Santa." Santa was my parents' ice-man and my father found it difficult to laugh at that observation, which was almost certainly intended to be taken as a joke.

My mother had five children in eight years, all Caesarian births at a time when that procedure was major surgery. After the birth of her last baby, she became a woman obsessed with her weight, one of the first people in our little Alaskan town to use the powdered diet food of the 1960s, Metracal. Her body seemed ludicrous to me when I was small, always ripening, bulging and healing, then sagging and flopping after yet another birth. Puberty felt like a death sentence to me when I began to lose my little child's body. I knew that meant the battle had begun—to keep from turning into my mother.

She was a woman who seemed shackled when I was young, although she would have hated that description. We owned two horses that she never rode, we lived near a beach that she went to once a year. When we moved to the unsettled area that she loved, it was a rare day that she insisted upon going for a walk by herself. Except the interludes in her car, she was a house-bound person with three indulgences, her coffee that she drank black by the quart, her phonograph records, and her books. Every night, after supper was over, my mother fell into a book and for a few hours left the demands of her housework, her husband, and her brood of insistent children.

She puzzled me when I was little. I had no idea of who this woman was. I used to lie awake at night, listening to my parents talk in the adjoining room, greedily trying to piece together what she liked, what she did when I wasn't around, what emotions she felt other than her frequently displayed and volatile temper. Tantalizing pieces of information floated past, eluding my comprehension but filed away in my memory. One night I heard a neighbor tell my father that he was in love with my mother and sometimes I heard her laugh.

I used to think she was beautiful and told her so at random moments, when she was brushing her hair, when she crooned endearments to her dog, on the very few times that she would dress up and go out with my father. A true New York girl, she always wore black, always with a dash of turquoise even if it was only her eye shadow. She treasured a pair of high-heeled shoes made of deep red leather and her camel's hair coat, which she wore on special occasions proudly, as though they were medals of honor.

She claimed not to care about her looks; vanity wasn't encouraged in our household. But she had a drawer that we called "the makeup drawer," cluttered with lipsticks in varying shades of scarlet, mascara that came in a solid block with a little brush, and a tiny pot of eye shadow that was applied no more frequently than once a year. When I showed a friend a photo of my family that had been taken when I was very small, she zeroed in on my mother immediately. "What a coquette," she said.

And that she was, a natural flirt who never admitted to it. Perhaps she never knew. She often told me "I don't like women," and the people who came to visit her were usually "the bachelors." In 1950's Alaska, the number of unmarried men was staggering and the ones in our tiny community gravitated to my mother. They'd sit and drink coffee and talk for hours while my father was gone on one of his summer construction jobs. One of them, a short, jolly, and rather religious Aleut, sent her a box of Whitman's Samplers for Christmas every year. We never knew why.

My mother enjoyed the company of men; she came from a family of three children, the older sister to twin boys. Her father, whom she adored, had left them in favor of a mistress; in those days divorce was a blazing scandal but a discreet mistress was socially accepted.

Her mother was perhaps the worst woman in the world to be a single parent, a "University Woman" whose father had permitted her to attend a Boston acting school after she had graduated with a degree that would allow her to teach children. She only received his permission by making a promise that once she had completed her training, she would never go on stage again.

The theatrical impresario, David Belasco saw my grandmother perform in her last role, before she abandoned acting forever. He was impressed and asked to meet her, but she had a promise to keep. That she stuck to her vow was probably a tragedy for everyone. She would have been a fine actress; she was a dreadful mother.

Trickles of her legacy were evident in her only daughter, who was a mixture of New England restraint that had been hardened over three centuries in a small town in Maine, and a volcanic Irish temper that was an ordinary drama in our household. "Please come in," I said graciously to one of "the bachelors" when he appeared at our door one day, "Mommy and Daddy are fighting." Nobody could say "You swine" quite as chillingly as my mother, always in a quiet voice but with deep disgust. She seldom used a stronger epithet but this one was blood-curdling. I still can't bring myself to say it.

"If we were twenty at the same time, we would never be friends," I told my mother the year before I was married at twenty-one. "Why do you say that?" she asked and it was one of the few times that I heard her sound hurt, without the usual accompanying rage. When I married, she was horrified, although I was only several years younger than she had been when she and my father wedded. I sometimes wondered if her nuptials had made her mother take to her bed; my mother collapsed into a blazing headache and paroxysm of violent nausea when she was told I had a husband.

My marriage was nothing like hers. My life was as little like hers as I could make it. Even as she grew old, she still provided an anti-model for me. Until the end of her life, I was certain that was the greatest gift my mother had ever given me, but I would learn that I was wrong.

"Where did you come from?" she asked me more than once during our life together. The question never offended me. Even as an adult, I thought of it as my own personal report card that measured my progress in my life-long work of not being my mother.

Chapter Three

Some people are better parents after their children are grown. I think I am and certainly my mother was with me—or perhaps I was a better child once I became an adult. The books, thoughts, and curiosity that we both loved we didn't really enjoy together until after I had turned fifty. I think that was when she finally had time—my father was dead, she no longer worked, and she was able to relax and savor the pleasures that had been crowded out by duty in her younger years. Frequently escaping to Reno, Seattle, Anchorage with my youngest sister—my mother claimed that her seventies were good years and I think that they may have been her best.

Five children in eight years is a life that I could never begin to fathom. There were five years between my sons and they still exhausted me in that first year of being a mother of two. The births that my mother went through were major surgery—trips to Anchorage for prenatal check-ups because the basic hospital in Homer wasn't capable of handling Caesarian births, a lengthy time afterward to recover, (it took over a week before she was allowed "to dangle" her feet over the edge of her bed), another Anchorage trip with the new baby that consisted of a complicated series of check-ups for both of them.

I was the child who had the luxury of living alone with my parents for over two years. There was a similar gap between the third and fourth children, but just a little over a year between the second and third, the fourth and fifth. Then my mother was told there could be no more babies.

Part One
What She Wanted

In addition to the physical and emotional depletion of complicated births, she had a husband who was legally blind and spent most of his energy trying to keep up on a construction site with men who were able to see, trying to do well at jobs that would allow his family to make it through the winter. When he came home, he expected recognition for his labors and heaven knows he got it. Until we were old enough to be helpful, taking care of him for nine months of every year was my mother's job.

And she was disappointed. Her obsessive dream from the time she was seven years old had been to live in Alaska. What she got was vastly different from the books she had read about the far north—Anchor Point in Southcentral Alaska, a small community of people from the Pacific Northwest who had never seen a ballet or an opera, who had no idea of where my mother came from or why she valued music or books. Her life was *The Egg and I* without the chuckles, and she was only in her twenties when she first stepped into her slightly curdled dream.

Within four years she had three children, all under the age of six, a washtub, a rudimentary kitchen, and an outhouse. Then everything she had brought with her to Alaska was consumed in a house fire, all of her books and records and family treasures that she and her husband had packed into a small trailer and transported from New York and Alaska by jeep. Later she told me, "I was on one side of a wall of fire and your father and you children were on the other." She ran to us through the flames and carried the scars on her arms for years before they finally faded away.

After their cabin was destroyed, my parents gave up their homesite and found a house beside the only road in the area. It was within walking distance of the post office and the grocery store, an essential location for my mother, who hadn't yet learned to drive. My father would go off to work on a construction project and was often gone for three months at a time, leaving my mother with three little girls in a place where she still felt terribly alone.

There were babies who didn't make it. I don't know how many miscarriages she had; she told me about two of them. Once again, just the physical drain alone from that must have been horrible. While still a very young woman, she was often a single parent for summers on end, tired, and living a life she had never planned on having. She bought us rubber boots, little yellow slickers and Maine fishermen's rain hats and sent us outdoors to play for hours, as soon as the youngest of us could walk. On the rare occasions that I had to bother her for something, I often found her locked in a deep sleep, angry when I woke her up.

Then once again she left us for Anchorage to have every tooth in her mouth pulled, as a precautionary measure. They were perfect but she showed the beginnings of gum disease and this, in Alaska of the 1950s, was the solution. Now she was a woman who was not yet thirty, with a complete set of dentures.

Every so often we'd talk and I learned the joy of chat. My mother was very lonely—and busy, and depressed, and doubtlessly homesick for Manhattan. Every year she tacked up a photo from a magazine of the Christmas tree at Rockefeller Center, even though she was surrounded by spruce trees, and our own Christmas tree, to my eyes, was magnificent.

Her daughters used to make bitter fun of the truth that although we grew up on a homestead, we never learned the skills that other women in our community passed on to our friends. Canning, sewing, gardening were alien to our household. But the women who practiced those domestic talents could have given birth in their potato fields, and they had able-bodied husbands. My mother needed just about every scrap of energy she had simply to keep us all healthy and nourished.

She did that surprisingly well, with a style and snap that went beyond the ordinary. She always rallied to make birthdays, Thanksgiving, Christmas, and Easter special, and they were much better than that. She made them magical. When she could dredge up the ability to sparkle and find the joy in life, nobody did that better.

She was a happier woman after her final baby was born, but soon afterward my father's eyesight began to get worse. He could no longer see our faces clearly and he began to fall into the depressions that would often turn him into a threatening stranger, a man who was bipolar. His highs made him great company, but at his lowest, he became violent toward his children.

He never touched my mother. He didn't have to. The life they had together was enough to persistently slap her in the face. She didn't break free until long after I was in my own home, with my own children. In the years before she left my father and found an apartment and a job in San Francisco, I was too busy to be the friend she longed for me to be. Her visits felt intrusive and the ones I made to her were obligatory. Not until we were both middle-aged women did we find our common ground.

Rashoman is never more true than when applied to family memories. None of us when recalling our parents are reliable observers. We each carry our own prisms that we form during childhood and that never leave us. I don't know the truth about my mother. None of her children do. Her parents and both of her brothers are dead, but I doubt that they knew her any better than we did. And now none of us will.

Hanging on to who she was for each of us, the best we can do is piece those memories together and hope they make a quilt. For me, I think of the young woman in a jeep, her baby in her lap, husband by her side, followed by a trailer full of things she treasured, heading North.

Mushroom hunting in Denali Park, 1951

Part One
What She Wanted

The cabin by the lake, 1952

Light and Silence

Chapter Four

In her last days, after she had moved from her Fairbanks apartment to the house where she would die, my mother asked to see her cat. In a little space the size of Van Gogh's bedroom, confined to lying on her back, that was all she asked for. She knew she couldn't keep him, she only wanted a visitation. This came close to breaking my heart.

Her life was measured in weeks and she was being given hospice care. Any drugs that she needed in any quantities were hers. Considering how she had hated drugs all of her life, this was ironic. Her life was ending with things she never wanted, and little of what she had always yearned for: privacy, a room with a view, the ability to take care of herself.

My mother was always a person of longing, never setting solid goals. When something she dreamed of came close to her grasp, she seized it. She always drifted into money, as though it were a magical substance, and when it melted, she usually, somehow, eventually, bumped into more.

Her own mother had an inborn respect for capital. "I dare not touch that money," she told a friend who once asked her for a loan, "that's my dead wood." Her daughter blithely and generously spent every cent that she ever had; money in her eyes was intended to make life comfortable. Unfortunately, she passed that belief down to me.

Slowly she stopped wanting and yearning, or at least she stopped voicing her desires. She stopped drinking coffee, which had always been her life's blood. She stopped eating chocolate. She stopped eating. The one hunger that she persistently satisfied was her voracious appetite for reading.

In old age, my mother spent her time becoming very Buddhist, separating herself from her desires. This was also very New England, which was probably more to the point. My mother had always wanted to be New England, not Irish. The confident, brash young man who told my grandmother when she refused to dance with him, "Miss Wescott, I'm going to marry you," and his family were people my mother loved, but they took second place. I never visited Patchogue to see where the Meehan stronghold had been, but my mother took us all to Maine where we trotted through the Wescott's ancestral house to see and do homage to its layers of history.

My mother always was sure she wouldn't live much past fifty and that fear was confirmed when high blood pressure struck her hard in her mid-thirties. "The doctor just told me that if I were a man, I would have already had a coronary," she told me when I was twelve, and from that moment her dread became my own.

No wonder she pushed the duties of "responsibility" upon me as soon as I could begin take them. In her vision of the future, she would be a tender memory and I would take over the household. She began to prepare me to be a back-up mother from the time I was ten and I reluctantly stepped in when I was needed for eight years.

When I was sixteen, we lived in Puerto Rico for a while, where my father tried to set up a boat-building business and my parents rented a dilapidated house on the outskirts of Mayaguez. We were befriended by a widower and his children; the oldest daughter, who was close to my age, filled the maternal gap.

"What if you couldn't ever go away to school or leave your brother and sisters?" my mother asked me one afternoon, as we sat on the verandah, watching mangos drop from a nearby tree.

"I suppose there could be a nuclear bomb that would wipe out the rest of the world and we would all have to band together," I replied with sixteen-year-old drama.

"I was thinking more of what happened to Eva," she replied.

My stomach churned violently as I thought of becoming the oldest Torres daughter, cooking, cleaning, caretaking, with all of the duties of being a woman and none of the privileges. I turned away from my mother and began to cultivate being a teenager who was so rebellious that nobody in her right mind would ever think of turning her into the angel on the hearth.

My father's business venture failed, we returned to Alaska, and my mother found a job in the office of a local entrepreneur. She loved having an independent, sociable life of her own, but without her presence during the day, our house felt empty. I did as little as necessary to make up her absence while she was at work, and my little brother and sister were left to their own amusements after school, "running wild," my father said. When I went off to college, he exerted his paternal authority, the family moved back to Anchor Point, and my mother was confined to domestic pursuits once again.

When she had a chance to break free, she grabbed it. She and my father cut up their homestead into 10-acre tracts. Fifty acres was divided among their children, the other hundred and ten were turned into a subdivision and put up for sale.

As the acreage sold, my mother traveled, first with my father, then by herself. She fell in love with San Francisco and made her home there. When rent increases forced her out of the city, she followed my sister and her husband to the interior of Alaska. She worked as long as she could; she bought, she spent, she gave.

An old lady friend of hers died and left her money to my mother, who gleefully burned her way through the legacy. When that was gone, so was the last piece of her subdivided homestead. She approached the end of her life with nothing—and in a way, I salute her for that. But then of course I would.

Part One
What She Wanted

In Anchor Point, among her few friends who still lived there, my mother was almost legendary. She came, she stayed apart, and then she left, always on her own terms. In that little town, she was given the status of a saint, unassailable, incomprehensible, and good. Anchor Point never knew that at heart she never really felt at home there, even though it was the only part of Alaska that was truly hers.

The house we moved to after the fire, 1953

Chapter Five

My mother's outer character was all I knew, and I knew it far too well. Much of what I saw in her she had passed on to me. Her legendary lack of balance and physical coordination made my own life a schoolyard hell. "Oh I guess we'll have to take you," one of my friends would say reluctantly and realistically while choosing a team for dodgeball or soccer, knowing that I was certain to guarantee ignominious defeat. Like my mother, I pretended it didn't matter. Now that I'm aging, I know from her example that balance can be a matter of life or death as I grow old.

My preference for men over women friends throughout my life is another inheritance from her that I'm paying for now. Women like my mother and me thought it was our dazzling wit and keen intellect that drew men to us for years, and that we responded in kind to their own internal attributes. But in truth once sexual attraction, voiced or unvoiced, left the equation, men to me became much more boring than women. It's just my tough luck that I never worked at making or keeping female friends. As I age, I long for them, but it's too late.

I'm rather certain that my mother discovered the same thing after sixty. She never had a significant male presence in her life after that particular birthday, and at forty, I didn't understand that at all. When my mother mentioned that Constance Helmerick's husband lived in Fairbanks as a widower, and that she had always harbored a vague attraction for him when she had read his wife's books about Arctic life, I urged her to contact him. She laughed, brushed it off, and never engineered an introduction, as far as I know. She still enjoyed male attention, but she had stopped seeking it. Now I know why.

My mother and I shared a passionate wish for solitude, privacy, and independence, while living in the same geographic area as our children. Like my mother, I found my home in Bangkok, as she had in San Francisco, and then learned that I couldn't live with seeing my children for only a week or two once a year. And like my mother, it was much easier for me to be distant in every sense from my maternal parent than it was from my offspring.

Improvidence was another link between my mother and me. Money came, money went, in a magical lunar cycle for us, like tides in an ocean We both had been horribly indebted to credit cards at one point in our lives, we spent what came our way with a joyful disregard for any future, we seemed to believe that money spent on other people didn't count as a real expenditure. We felt certain that a 401K was a lousy waste of money that could otherwise take us to Europe/Asia/Africa/Dubuque. We hungered for tickets—any kind, to any place—and late in life we both exhibited an expensive yearning for comfortable, pretty living spaces.

If it hadn't been for my years in Thailand, where I finally learned how to eat, food would have been another issue I continued to share with my mother. Her love/hate relationship with nourishment grew deeper and more deadly as she approached ninety. A preoccupation with weight had made her think of food as a substance to fear—or at least be wary of—not to enjoy. Food intake is the first form of power that any child learns and my mother had never moved beyond that.

Until I lived in Bangkok, I mirrored her obsession. When events felt most out of control, I could always control what I ate and how much. Still no matter how small my body became, it was never the way I wanted it. I was an ideal candidate for anorexia and my mother was too, although I don't think she ever practiced that particular art of starvation. It makes me sad to think that she spent the last decade of her life denying herself the pleasure of eating things she liked. When I learned that near the end, from her bed she had asked my sister if she had brought a batch of freshly baked cookies,

I had a flare of hope that my mother just might stay alive for another year or two.

Our gluttony had always been reserved for books. We stocked up on them the way Mormons did a ten-year food supply. We lusted after books; we coveted them; we devoured them. The difference between us was I had to learn to live without them, at a rough financial point during my time in Thailand, and without them I began to write.

My mother never was deprived of reading material. Even when we moved back into the hills, my father would bring us the mail once a week or so and it was always a heavy load. My mother subscribed to almost every magazine in existence: *Life, Time, The Saturday Evening Post, Ladies Home Journal, McCall's, Good Housekeeping.*

At that time print was king and television was still an adjunct. Writers, sometimes good ones, were serialized in magazines; novels arrived in installments once a month. *Life* had columnists who were provocative handlers of prose and sometimes an entire issue would be devoted to one writer. Copies of *National Geographic* and the *New Yorker* were treasured when my mother could afford them; when I was fourteen I delved into her five-foot stack of old *New Yorkers* and found Muriel Spark and J.D. Salinger. No matter how poor we were, we always had something to read, because of my mother.

And she trained me to be a traveler. In territorial Alaska, planes were our Greyhound bus system and my mother loved to fly. She taught me to be thrilled at takeoffs and landings; she taught me that tickets were magic carpets, and I would beg for used ones when she or my father came back from a trip. She taught me to value those bits of paper in a way that neither of us ever did money. Currency had value for us only because it could take us on a journey.

We both loved clothes. We both were frequently unkind to our children. We both chased a dream and much later regretted what that had done to people we loved. We both in many ways were very selfish women.

Part One
What She Wanted

And yet we both always tried as hard as we could to be better parents than our own mothers had been to us.

Building furniture was a family project, with even Nushnik involved, 1954

Part Two
What She Gave

Chapter Six

My mother cared for us with a benign but unimaginative neglect that could only be practiced by a woman with urban sensibilities. We were surrounded by hazards so far from any context she had ever experienced that for her they didn't exist. She was a woman whose idea of roughing it for most of her life had been a few romantic years of living with a bathtub in the kitchen of a Manhattan walk-up when she was a newlywed. How could she be expected to understand the perils that lurked in wait for very small girls in an outdoor privy?

We were visiting a gigantic bachelor who had an outhouse large enough to accommodate his bulk, when one of my little sisters almost plunged to a fate worse than death. I ran into our host's cabin shrieking "Hurry! Hurry! She's falling down the outhouse hole!" My father and his friend tore off to the rescue, finding my youngest sister desperately clinging to the victim's hands, trying to keep her from sliding inch by inch toward her doom.

Shortly after her narrow escape, my sister created a character named Georgie Pewstinker who lived at the bottom of an outhouse hole. Her portraits of this creature would make her a prime candidate for a child therapist nowadays, but my parents found her spurt of imagination completely amusing. A visitor from the states put Georgie Pewstinker into a poem and he became one of the family, frequently channeled by my sister. He spoke in a bloodcurdling yodel with long drawn-out syllables, which was probably quite cathartic.

Part Two
What She Gave

A year or two later, when I had just embarked upon my academic career, I was dressed, brushed, and ready for school, a one-room educational institution that was just a few steps down the road that ran in front of our house. It was a gorgeous day with a fresh snowfall and I decided I wasn't in the mood to waste all of this in a classroom, which was beginning to be a little dull. I launched myself into one of the silent scenarios that I could role play for hours—Anne Bonney the pirate was a particular favorite.

My little sisters must have been sick that day or else they would have noticed me floating about in the snow, stick-sword in hand, quietly dueling with an invisible opponent. But nobody saw me, until my teacher walked past our house on her way home at lunch time.

"What are you doing? Go to school right now," she demanded and I pulled myself out of my buccaneer existence, arriving at school just in time for recess.

My mother never knew about my truancy but my teacher began to invite me to her house on Saturday to spend the afternoon making doughnuts with her. I loved the attention and she seemed to think that I needed it.

When we moved away from town to our house in the hills, we became a bit isolated from the rest of the world and slowly we began to recreate a life that I'd later recognize in *Lord of the Flies* and *A High Wind in Jamaica*, a society of semi-feral children. Because we had been imbued with a rigorous infusion of "company manners," we behaved well enough in our rare social encounters but in our daily lives we were savages.

One summer, a boy we knew came to stay for a month. This was a common custom in our homestead culture; when my mother had begun to have more children, I'd been farmed out on a regular basis to friends of my parents from the time I was two.

My sisters and I didn't really like Martin. He was a spoiled brat with a mean streak but he had a rebellious *joie de vivre* that eventually won us over. He had useful talents that we hadn't yet acquired; he was good with a knife and he had brought his own little hatchet.

There was a huge thicket of alder bushes quite close to our house and we found that once we were inside that enclosure, we were invisible. The branches were so dense around and above us that we could see nothing but green. Even when it rained, the canopy of bushes kept us from getting soaked. It was the perfect place to do whatever we wanted, whenever we wished, for hours without interruption.

"Let's make a city, or at least an apartment building," I suggested. "We can each have our own private chamber."

For weeks, we worked at clearing small spaces within the jungle. Martin hacked away vigorously with his hatchet and I found that if I stripped the butchered alder branches of bark and leaves, they became whips. My sisters and I made many of them which we stacked neatly in our chambers.

Martin's father knew a man who had undergone the Bataan Death March, a story that might not be every child's idea of an adventure worth having, but it appealed to Martin. Once he told it to us, we realized it had possibilities, but we identified with the captors, not the war heroes. Slowly a plan took shape.

There was a group of children whom we detested who lived down the hill. They were slow of speech and had no spark; we were convinced they were of another species, definitely below the animal kingdom. We would never have done to animals what we had in store for the Smith children.

Whips weren't enough. Martin chopped down thorny stalks of devil's club and we put on our winter mittens to carry them to our torture chambers. When we had enough, we knew it was time to carry out our plan.

"Come and play with us," we invited the Smiths, "It's such an exciting game—you'll see." They willingly tagged along as we left their yard and as soon as all adults were out of sight, we sternly put our captives in parade formation.

"Get in a straight line," I barked and Martin flourished his hatchet. The two of us led the way, my sisters bringing up the rear, and shouts of "Hup two three four! Move it!" rang through the wilderness.

The Smiths looked worried and the smallest began to cry. "What's this game called?" one of them asked and Martin replied, "This is a Death March."

"Yes," my youngest sister said, "We're going to torture you in the alder patch."

I glared at her. "We told you not to tell them that. It's a surprise."

The oldest Smith broke ranks and began to sprint with speed spawned by adrenaline and terror. Martin and I were reluctant to abandon our remaining prisoners. We sent my sisters in pursuit, but it was too late. Before they caught her, Mildred Smith made it into our house, shrieking "Help, help! They're going to kill us."

"Of course we didn't say that," we all lied repeatedly, "It was just a game."

The Smiths went home and the chambers in the alder thicket slowly disappeared. Before Martin left us, he managed to split his forehead open with a vigorous swing of his hatchet and sported a rakish bandage for the rest of his stay. In a burst of the rivalry that existed between us, I sliced my foot rather deeply with an axe while trying to chop wood on a slow afternoon.

It was undoubtedly karmic retribution for the devil's club, but we failed to absorb the moral lesson conveyed by our bloodshed. Even without Martin, our amusements were unconventional and creative.

Once my foot healed, my sisters and I engaged two neat and prissy visitors in a spirited battle that owed quite a bit to a snowball fight, although it took place in June. We were all feeling bored and even Billy and Martha agreed that a spot of combat would liven things up. It had been raining and mud was easy to come by. We made many, many gooey projectiles, took up our attack positions, and fired.

Our resourcefulness won no plaudits when our parents had finished their lengthy conversation and came out to find us. Neither our household nor that of our guests had inside plumbing and five children dripping with mud weren't what any adult without a bathtub would care to find at the end of the day.

After that we all played at Billy and Martha's house, where their mother cut our sandwiches into neat diamond shapes and encouraged us to stay indoors. We busied ourselves in one of the bedrooms with Martha's dolls, all of us enthralled for hours. Even Billy joined in once he saw what the game was all about. Their mother was pleased until the day she asked "Why are you playing in the dark?" and learned that we were playing Murder.

The plot that we related to her was much too lurid and grisly for her tastes and Martha and Billy learned to live without our company. Somehow we bore up under the deprivation. We were too busy to care; we had just learned to play cards. I'd recently read about Las Vegas and gambling for a penny a point was taking up all of our attention. With a little practice, I told my sisters, we could probably start a kid's casino.

Me in the fireweed, 1954

Part Two
What She Gave

Devil's Club in the woods

Nushnik's unsuccessful career as a sled dog, 1955

Chapter Seven

We never had running water and only sporadically had electricity, but we were never without a matched pair of Seal Point Siamese cats, who were always called Daphne and Gilmore. My mother had christened the first pair and their successors continued to carry on the tradition. Although she was a demon for shortening Christian names, rather like her Maine forbears who would christen a daughter Proserpine and then call her Prossy, my mother always addressed Daphne and Gilmore formally. Somehow it would have been sacrilege to call them Daff and Gill.

They were descendents of Anna Fisheye, who had the bad fortune to be named by me. An imperious Siamese kitten with a commanding language of meows and purrs, she had ridden into town on the shoulder of one of the bachelors, when he drove to our little Alaskan community from Chicago. We all were enchanted by her at first sight and my mother told her owner that when Anna was old enough to have kittens, we would take two of them, male and female.

I don't know if Anna's owner had thought about breeding her. She was still very little, and I suppose that they were both recovering from her arduous journey north. But Joe adored my mother, and somehow when Anna was old enough, a purebred Seal Point Siamese male came to call upon her on an extended visit.

Heaven only knows how Joe had found Anna's mate in 1950's territorial Alaska. It was a rough country then; most people kept cats as mousers and dogs as transportation. Sleds pulled by huskies were a common sight in winter and Joe soon had a dog sled and team himself. But before that he found the father of Anna's kittens and brought him home.

That alone must have been quite the little odyssey. This cat was massive; he would have turned Joe into a hunchback if he had perched on the man's shoulders and his personality was far from cuddly. Before his mission was accomplished, he would stalk the woods at night near our house and scream for food. He would perch on the windowsill and peer in at us with a baleful stare; my mother called him Mephistopheles.

I wanted to keep him but once his job was completed, he returned home. After beginning his dynasty, he was never needed again. Anna Fisheye obligingly produced both male and female kittens, and two of them became the first of the Daphnes and Gilmores.

I think my mother had vague dreams of making some pin money by raising Siamese cats. Other women in our area chose chickens as a way to supplement their household money but that was too mundane for her. She was a woman of original ideas that were never encumbered by marketing plans.

Anna Fisheye had produced six kittens. It was reasonable to assume that her daughter would do the same. We lived in a village of 98 people, which at best meant 25 families. Even if each household was willing to purchase a purebred Siamese kitten, which was doubtful since barn cats could be had for nothing, that market would be saturated after three litters. Nevertheless, Daphne and Gilmore grew up, vigorously and regularly reproduced, and the kittens moved on. We never asked where they went.

The Siamese cats were a much more enduring enterprise than the Flemish Giant rabbits that my father bought, built hutches for, and bred. They were intended for food, not profit, but the first time we sat down for supper, asked what was on our plates, and were foolishly told "Rabbit," the three of us burst into wild sobs. We were never served rabbit again but that winter we ate quite a bit of "chicken." Then the rabbits all died and my father's next foray into the realm of utilitarian animals was a team of sled dogs.

There were eight of them, and each came with his own doghouse. They set up camp far beyond our backyard where we played every day and we were sternly forbidden to go anywhere near them. It was a fairly routine occurrence for children to be mauled by sled dogs, my father told us. They were dangerous and shouldn't be thought of as pets.

What my father hadn't been told was that one of them actually had been someone's pet, even if he'd never achieved the honor of becoming a house dog. I was convinced he liked me and often assured my father that Sitka was a good guy, not a savage beast. This theory only produced another batch of horrific tales about children who were hideously scarred by the fangs of sled dogs.

My father practiced his dog-mushing skills until finally he decided that it was safe to take his three little girls for a sled ride. Bundled up like small Siberian peasants, we were placed in the sled, my father shouted "Mush" and we began to move. The runners squeaked in the new snow, the dogs panted happily, and all three of us began to sing "Jingle Bells." We were living the dream until somehow the long harness that linked the dogs became tangled, the sled stopped, and my father waded into the canine confusion to put things to rights.

Sitka was the wheel dog, the last in line and the closest to us. Finding that he was the only dog not in caught up in the tangled mess, he seized his chance. He rushed toward us and happily began to nuzzle our faces with obvious affection. We responded with pats and endearments until my father looked up. "I saw him near your heads and I was sure the next thing I saw would be three little girls without noses," he told us later.

We were desolate when he put Sitka back to work and we cried all the way home.

"Sitka loves us," I argued, "Why can't he be my dog?"

"We already have a dog," my mother replied, "Nushnik would kill Sitka if you brought him in the house. What's wrong with you? Don't you love Nushnik anymore?"

Part Two
What She Gave

That was a low blow. We all adored Nushnik, a huge mixture of German Shepherd, Siberian Husky, and Saint Bernard. He had been my best friend since I was three; by the time he was six months old, he was taller than I when he was in a sitting position, and I thought of him as my big brother. He was so gentle that even Daphne and Gilmore's kittens played with him, but he was savagely territorial. Other dogs quickly learned to stay off his turf and away from his children. He would have killed Sitka; I knew that, but I still felt the bitter injustice of Nushnik receiving all of our affection while Sitka was heartbroken in his miserable dog house.

I couldn't do anything about this until break-up, when the snow melted and it was warm enough to sit outdoors. Then I'd take my copy of *White Fang* to a tree near the doghouses and read aloud until my voice got tired. The sled dogs watched me attentively, not only Sitka but even the ones who had never become my friends. When I would turn to leave, they'd still be sitting, heads cocked to one side, looking eager with their husky grins. Usually I went back to give them one more chapter.

It was the best I could do. They seemed to enjoy it and I hoped they didn't miss it too much when my father decided that dog-mushing was too much work and sold them all.

They were followed by goats because one of my sisters was allergic to cow's milk, but they were never truly attractive pets, although we tried to love them. They smelled and they were stupid animals. We never asked if we could bring them in the house.

Then the true stars of the animal kingdom came into our lives.

When I was ten, a man named Stinky Jones sold my father two horses, Rondo and Ranger. They were of no determinate breed; they were pack horses, sturdy and graceless, but they were the granting of a wish I'd had since my father had read *Black Beauty* aloud. I loved everything about them: their rich, grassy smell, the warmth of sunlight on their backs, the smooth lap of their tongues when I put sugar on my outstretched palm, their beautiful kind eyes. I loved the tack that came with them, bridles, horse collars, an old McClellan saddle that dated back to the days when some of our army was still truly cavalry.

A neighbor gave me an old saddle he had lying around that was just my size. I polished it with saddle soap and learned how to cinch it tight— horses had the cool joke of inflating their bellies with air when they were being saddled, then releasing it later so the whole thing would slip sideways, along with the rider. I always tapped Ranger's belly with my bony little knee as a matter of form; he never seemed to notice. He had another joke in store for me, which was to head for the nearest tree branch that hung low enough to scrape me off his back.

He probably had never been ridden as much as I demanded of him. He was a horse that had been used during moose hunting season to carry gear into the back country. He'd been forced to walk a trail without deviation and now he had a lighter load on his back than he'd probably ever had before, with no trail to follow. When the tree-scraping trick no longer worked, he began to crow-hop when I got on his back. This delighted me no end— "Look, he's bucking!" Finally we settled in together and I was in heaven.

The horses? Not so much. They had an uncanny way of knowing when they would be needed and on that morning they would disappear. It was my job to go out with a halter, a rope, and a can of oats, on a sort of Easter egg hunt, searching for them. They were good at hiding but I would hear the odd little burbling sound that they made with their lips or catch sight of a flicker of Rondo's blonde hide shimmering from a patch of trees. One of them would always succumb to the sound of swishing oats and he would be the one who would wear the halter. The other, with a distinct air of reluctant disgust, would follow behind. They were a matched set, those boys.

They hated any kind of labor. Quickly they became part of our animal tribe, along with the dogs, the Siamese cat couple, and the batches of kittens. They received the same affection and attention and it didn't take long for them to notice that they were the only animals who actually worked once in a while. They resented that as much as they did the sad truth that they couldn't come in the house. In the summer it was a common sight to see one of them with his head and shoulders inside the kitchen door, watching my mother cook.

Rondo was there when she put a pumpkin pie on the counter to cool and he discovered that if he craned his neck far enough, he could reach it. And he did, with immense enjoyment. My mother turned to find my little brother paralytic with laughter and most of the pie gone. She swatted Rondo away with a broom and he looked at her benignly as he retreated. He knew she wasn't really angry. None of us were ever angry with the horses.

They were the kindest animals who ever lived with us, even if their senses of humor occasionally left something to be desired. Their hiding was a game; they never went very far from the house and they always let me find them. It wasn't their fault that they concealed themselves near meadows where the grass grew higher than my head and soaked through my underwear on rainy days. As I shivered my way back to the house, horses in tow, I was often nudged by big, velvet noses. "You win this time," their soft eyes seemed to say.

When Ranger died, Rondo in many ways crossed over. He was less a horse and more one of the dogs, who accepted him without reservation. My little brother and sister rarely rode him, and I think he liked them best because of that. With them he was what he wanted to be, a large friendly animal who didn't have to do any sort of labor. He'd move toward them, with the dogs and the cats, never stepping on the kittens, looking for food and attention and love.

In this wild whirl of animals that came and lived with us and then died, the Daphnes and Gimores were fixed points. They loved us, slept with us, had adorable babies, and when they passed on, they were replaced by another Daphne, another Gilmore. To hell with rabbits, goats, even sled dogs— Nushnik of course didn't count. He wasn't a pet; he was one of the kids and of all of us, I knew he was my mother's favorite.

And why not? He adored her, he obeyed her, and he never talked back. His life was enviable, we all understood, because he was good. Sitka, I sometimes thought, should have been so lucky.

Me riding Rondo in the Ninilchik Rodeo Parade, 1960

Part Two
What She Gave

Mountains of Kachemak Bay, near Homer

Light and Silence

Chapter Eight

Eating would have been an irksome chore when I was growing up, if my mother hadn't learned to bake. Limited by her available ingredients to preparing an endless string of meat and potato meals with a canned vegetable on the side, she became an indifferent cook. Probably because the meat she prepared was moose, she cooked it until it was a shade of opalescent grey, without the faintest trace of pink. Potatoes were customarily served in boiled chunks and the vegetables, although already cooked in the can, were boiled too. Lima beans provided an occasional diversion, soft, pillowy and flavorless, unless they were laced heavily with Tabasco sauce. I disliked them, but choked them down, grateful that they weren't the potatoes that were almost always on my plate.

The monotony of what she was given to prepare must have driven my mother to the brink. When she learned to bake bread, she at last found something she could enjoy. The alchemy of yeast and water and the dough coming to life under her hands, the magic of it puffing up in a bowl, the promising odor that came from it when she punched it down, and the socially sanctioned violence of kneading—I loved watching my mother bake bread when I was little. Her white hands working the dough, pressing, slapping, pushing it into elasticity, was a feat of legerdemain, a kind of performance art, and the delight of eating a piece of bread when it first came out of the oven was sharp and sensual. Melted margarine soaked into the soft core of the slice, the prickly chewiness of the crust—this was where I learned that eating could be a pleasure, not a duty.

Part Two
What She Gave

When the obligatory chewing was over at suppertime, the cake would appear—its layers covered with frosting that made what was underneath a surprise. Frosting was another magical occurrence—an uninteresting, pale mixture of powdered white sugar and a chunk of gleaming yellow margarine became transformed with a few drops of food coloring from a little, tear-shaped piece of plastic and a teaspoon of flavoring from a brown bottle that held the deep, warm fragrance of vanilla.

Before the other babies were born, my mother usually worked her alchemy unaccompanied. I was my father's daughter when I was small. One of the most potent sentences I learned to utter was "Can I go along?" Sometimes it was into the woods or down to a lake filled with waterlilies, but what I loved best was when we headed for the jeep and went visiting. The houses we went to belonged to the bachelors and they usually had an animal or two lying around. That was when I learned to make no distinction between animals and people. If I wanted somebody to play with, I had two choices. I could play with the animals or I could hang out with my best friend whom only I could see, Penelope Piddlepump.

At night my father would read to me, with great dramatic flair—a chapter or two from *Heidi* or *The Rose and the Ring*. Some nights we'd sing before I went off to bed. My mother had a lovely voice but I don't remember hearing it except at Christmas when we all sang carols. She was usually silent in the evenings after supper, while my father provided the entertainment.

Her life was already hard, even with only me as the resident child. She used a washboard to scrub our clothes clean and I was always afraid that her knuckles would bleed when I watched the terrible vigor with which she rubbed fabric against the metal ridges of the board.

But I knew that when she wasn't busy, my mother could make my life gleam with adventures. My father offered freedom but my mother had the gift of stories and transformations.

There were rare afternoons when she would show me old photographs pasted with gold corners onto stiff, black pages in albums, or we'd examine the contents of her jewel box, where I was enchanted by her baby bracelet.

It was too small for my wrist but I loved to hold it; it was smooth and gleaming sterling silver, like the little spoon and pusher from Tiffany's that I used every night when I ate my moose meat and boiled potatoes.

We were closest, my mother and I, on the days that she made gingerbread. She let me stand beside her on a chair and push the ingredients her way as she called them out to me—"molasses, flour, eggs." She allowed me to become part of her magic on those afternoons, a small sorcerer's apprentice. She gave me a reply to the words I hated, "You're a little girl." Now I could stand straight in defiance, chin up, and retort, "I'm not a little girl. I'm a big girl. I make gingerbread."

After our cabin burned to the ground, we never made gingerbread together again.

Christmas 1953

Part Two
What She Gave

The house my father built on the bluff, 1955

Light and Silence

Chapter Nine

My father built a new house for us after the fire. It was surrounded by trees, high on a bluff with a view of a river and the uninhabited hills that lined the horizon. The living room had big windows that framed that same view, and stairs led to the bedrooms above. I'd never seen stairs before and they were an exotic touch as far as I was concerned.

When we went out to play, we were immediately in the woods, with odd little paths that led nowhere and hillocks of bouncy green moss. Growths of fungus with flat, smooth, and slimy fronts protruded from the trunks of spruce trees, looking like something dinosaurs would have nibbled on. We found we could easily tear them from the trees and began to collect them in different sizes, some smaller than my smallest sister's hand, others the size of dinner plates. There was no use for them that we could discover. Although some women in our town dried them and painted little landscapes on their flat sides, my mother put those creative efforts in the same category as earrings made from dried moose droppings. "Basket weaving," she sniffed.

My father had recently read *Tom Sawyer* aloud and my deepest ambition was to find a cave. There were burrows in the moss hills and I was optimistic that someday there would be one large enough for me to enter and explore. I never found one, but the dream was enough to keep me searching for months.

Warm dirt under my feet meant the arrival of summer. My sisters and I ran barefoot from the minute the ground thawed until the first frost hit a few months later. The priest who visited once a month to say Mass in our living room told us that his mother had made him run barefoot in the first snow to keep him from having sore throats in the winter and we tried it once. It didn't work in Alaska.

We were happy in that house. My mother wasn't. One winter when my father still had the dog team, he took us to stay with a neighbor for the day and put my mother in the sled. They rode for hours, down a road, across the frozen swampland that we called muskeg, and up into the distant hills that we could see from our living room windows. The dogs panted their way up a long slope and my mother asked "Where are we going?" "Don't look back until I tell you," my father ordered.

At the top of the hill, he stopped the sled and told my mother to get out and turn around. It was a clear day and when she did as she was told, my mother saw below her the land they had just traveled through, bordered by miles of coastline. Beyond the water was a long range of mountains, one of them puffing out a ribbon of smoke, clearly a volcano. She was in love immediately; it was the best present my father ever gave her.

He had stopped the sled in an open sweep of clear land with two giant spruce trees nearby, which my mother promptly named the Sentinels. It was grassland, dotted with belts of trees. When my mother first saw this spot, it stretched before her in dazzling whiteness that twinkled with sparks of tiny colored lights if she stared at it long enough. The wind had blown the snow into dunes and put such a thick, hard crust on its surface that she could walk on top of it without falling through. She stood in the middle of a cold and glittering desert. "I want my house here," she said.

There was no road to this place, only a hunting trail that snaked through trees and swamps. In the winter, after freeze-up, vehicles could drive through the muskeg but when the ground thawed during break-up, it turned to a bog of mush that horses could sink in right up to their bellies. My father had to bring in building materials during the winter and then work on construction sites through the summer to be able to buy more. It was at least a year before my mother could move to the spot that she loved with a wild and truly unreasoning passion, and take possession of the Alaskan dream that she had longed for since childhood.

When the house was finally built, it was exactly where she wanted it, in the middle of an unending stretch of meadow with that regal view. It was two stories high, with a bank of windows running along its front that captured the mountains and framed the setting sun as it disappeared behind them at the end of a clear day. In the summer the grass grew higher than my father's head; except for groves of alders and an occasional well-placed birch tree, we were surrounded by a ripple of green. In the winter it was a windblown, stark glare of unbroken white.

My mother named her place Windswept after a favorite novel about a house on the coast of Maine; she was romantic that way. It was actually wind-rocked. It was too far from any trees to be given protection from the gale-force winds that came in from Cook Inlet and pummeled the house. It moved like a ship when there was a good storm, creaking and swaying the walls of our upstairs bedrooms.

The windows that my mother insisted upon were clear plastic when we moved in, not yet the glass that my father would earn on his next construction job the following summer. The plastic wasn't drawn taut, it billowed, and inside the house, each plastic sheet that would eventually become a front window was buttressed by crosses of thin strips of lath. They looked extremely ugly, but without them the plastic would have blown out in the first storm. Upstairs where the windows were smaller, but still larger than they probably should have been, they frequently did burst.

With a loud thunder crack, the wind came howling into a bedroom, we shrieked helpfully, and my parents rushed to the rescue with blankets, nails, and a hammer. Wind whistled through the blankets that were tacked over the open window, the house would shake under its force, and we burrowed deeper into our sleeping bags, cradled to sleep in a house that was out of place but refused to be blown away.

The house my father built was never completely finished. The bottom half of it was made of logs, but they were unpeeled. When the bark has been removed from building logs, the effect is charming, gleaming and golden like pieces of Crackerjack, but the process takes a very long time. I watched the parents of one of my friends painstakingly and carefully plane the bark from every log that went into their house. It took them all summer.

My father didn't take that time. Bark flaked from the walls of our downstairs for years until he and my mother soaked burlap sacks in buckets of whitewash and tacked them over the logs. It gave the somewhat disorienting feeling of the Southwest in southwestern Alaska, the smooth white cloth rolling over the logs in frozen ripples.

One summer, years before he built this house, a construction job that was only twenty miles from Anchor Point allowed my father the rare privilege of commuting from home. After the radar tower was built, there were leftovers—cement blocks and big sheets of wood and planks with nails protruding from them. My father brought these treasures home and stockpiled them. The sheets became the floor of our new house; they were thick and serviceable and they charmed us children because they were flawed with knot holes. When my parents weren't around, I found I could stuff an entire breakfast serving of scrambled eggs, fork by fork, down one of those knot holes without ever getting out of my chair.

The floors were never, of course, replaced. They took rustic to a whole other level, but my parents had enough panache to successfully ignore them.

The second story and the attic were made from lumber. Before the planks weathered, they shone almost as brightly as peeled logs upon our hill, a sight visible for miles in winter when the muskeg trail was frozen into usability again. As my father drove home on winter nights, the lights of our house glowed through the plastic-paned windows, beaming him safely back to us.

It was a house built with ingenuity, improvisation, and speed. It was a barn with impractical fenestration. It was a partially realized dream that never came completely true, and for decades after my family abandoned it, it remained a landmark, visible and commanding, on the empty hill.

My mother's house on the hill

Part Two
What She Gave

Homestead road near our house

Chapter Ten

When I was insufferably nineteen, I discovered Abraham Maslow's description of peak experiences and carefully explained what they were to the doddering old fool who was my father. When I condescendingly asked him if he had ever felt such a transcendent moment, he replied with far more honesty and respect than I deserved. "Yes, when I built this house for your mother and you children."

In a setting of breathtaking beauty, he and one of his friends had flung together a home for his family, ungainly and of mammoth proportions. It had the potential of magnificence, of a place for generations of family, and that's what my mother taught us to see when we looked at our house or thought about it.

As imperfect and unfinished as it was, it wasn't out of place among the houses of people we knew. Few in our community had electricity, and almost all had no inside plumbing. Many of our friends lived in houses much smaller than ours, temporary cabins in settings that were easy to reach, near a road or on flat land. The scant number of houses that approached normal levels of comfort had been built by the government in territorial days, to shelter people who worked for federal agencies, or else they had been constructed by bachelors who had no children to gobble up their summer earnings.

Our house represented months and months of my father's work. He had labored on construction sites and then hauled building materials across the frozen muskeg and up a steep hill that had no road. He and a friend had built a little shanty, a crude shelter with a couple of benches, a bunkbed, and a cheap stove where they could take a break or have a meal while they worked on the house. It was a place where they could warm up over a cup of coffee or stay if a storm blew up and they had to spend the night. They brought sleeping bags, a few pieces of kitchenware, a camp stove for cooking, and then they began to build.

Every one of those unpeeled logs had to be set into place; then the huge windows were cut out of the walls. After that the two men built the second story by hoisting up the timber and the thick narrow planks that formed the support for the floor. They topped the whole thing with a high, peaked roof and put down floor joists for the attic. And that was only the frame. There was much more work to come.

The next installment had to be postponed until the following winter, after my father made the money to buy the clear plastic that would cover the open window spaces cut into every wall of the house, or the pipes that would offer a rudimentary drain for the kitchen sink. He had to put in a heating system: a barrel stove, which was a 50-gallon drum with a door welded to one end and a hole cut on the side for the stove pipe. There was so much stove pipe; it ran through the center of the house up to the second story. Upstairs its length was broken by another 50-gallon drum that stood upright with more stove pipe leading into it and up to the roof. This served as a radiator for the sleeping area, which for the first year was one huge room.

The house wasn't ready until after New Year's that winter and to us children it seemed to have always been on the hill, waiting. But it had been spawned by work and it demanded work, from all of us. At first it was fun, settling in with our household furniture and staking the separate corners that would be our own rooms someday. We were wildly elated. Only my father knew how much hard labor waited for everybody.

My mother had of course been working ever since she arrived in Alaska, only recently emerging from the nineteenth century into some semblance of the twentieth. Our house in town finally had electricity that came from wires and poles, not a diesel generator with a hand crank. It had been heated by an ugly oil furnace, and the kitchen had a propane range with an oven that had replaced an old-fashioned woodstove. She had a wringer washer and when the clothes were clean, she didn't have to use heavy sad-irons to take out the wrinkles. She had an electric iron and an electric mixer and a phonograph with a large library of record albums that she ordered by mail by the carton from Sam Goody's catalogs.

In her new home she was back to preparing meals on a two-burner camp stove for our first winter. She had to put cloth mantles over the pipes in the Blazo lanterns, fill them with white gas, pump them so the fuel reached the mantles and then light each one just before darkness fell. Washing clothes became an aerobic exercise again and she learned to make English muffins that could go from raw dough to cooked bread on top of the barrel stove, no oven required.

Two of us had to be taken to school and that became an all-day job for my father. He swaddled my younger sister and me within blankets in the wooden rumble seat of a Ford tractor and drove us down the hill and across the muskeg. Our car was parked where our trail ended and the road into town began; we climbed out of our nest of sleeping bags and into the backseat. At the end of the day the procedure was reversed. We didn't miss as much school as we would have wanted, but then education took on a new luster when we learned that when we weren't in our classrooms, we had work to do.

It took a lot of wood to keep our house warm. My father brought a chainsaw and his little girls to the woods behind our house where he felled trees, built a bonfire from their large, heavy branches, and cut the trunks into round logs. It was our job to fill the rumble seat of the tractor with pieces of wood and unload it back at the house, over and over again, all day long.

It was exciting at first, with the falling trees crashing to the ground as we watched safely by our father's side, and the flames of the bonfire leaping high above our heads when my father threw a match into the pile of gasoline-soaked branches. But our feet got cold quickly, no matter how fast

Part Two
What She Gave

we moved with our loads of wood, and the whine of the chainsaw was as insistent and irritating as a dentist's drill. Sometimes we came too close as my father worked and little chunks of wood and bark that came out in the cloud of sawdust would sting us as they hit our faces. "Are we done yet?' we'd ask hopefully as we took another load of cut wood home and it took hours before my father finally said yes.

We got our drinking water from an underwater spring that my father had found; he chopped the ice away from its surface and we'd fill five-gallon water cans to bring home. Water for washing came from snow; we'd scoop it up in buckets and fill an empty 50-gallon drum with snow that melted to almost nothing. It took countless trips to bring in enough snow to give my mother the water she needed for washing dishes and as it melted it radiated winter through the downstairs of our house.

By the time I was ten, I had become a useful child and soon after that I turned into a scullery maid. I could peel potatoes and put them on the stove to boil for supper; I could bake a cake; I could take care of my sisters and brother in a pinch. I could even at times manage to turn the handle of the diesel generator with enough force that for a few hours we'd have electricity and when I couldn't, I learned to light the Blazo lanterns that frightened me beyond all reason. And as my mother began to take to her bed with nausea and blinding headaches, I learned how to worry.

In our new home, my mother had became a blazing supernova. Now that we lived in an area where there were only four families scattered over miles of hills, woods, and meadows, she took on an importance she had never possessed when we had other social touchstones. Then she got hepatitis, her eyes and skin turned yellow with jaundice, and she went away for an entire winter.

My little sister was sent off to stay with a German woman who had married Anna Fisheye's owner. The rest of us remained with my father in a weird little enclave that knew no rules. When my mother returned in the spring with gifts and restored health, we wanted to devour her, or at least embrace her with our engulfing closeness so tightly that she would never leave us again.

Light and Silence

She came back home crackling with New York energy. She moved differently. After months of convalescing with her own mother in a tiny one-bedroom Manhattan apartment, she was ready to reclaim her adventure.

She took charge of our education, sending away to the Calvert School in Maryland for books and instructional materials. My father built three little tables and put planks over Blazo boxes to serve as our desk chairs and every morning we sat in obedient expectation. We learned to write in a penmanship with no floss or flourishes; we pored over muddy reproductions of painted masterpieces for art appreciation; we wrote countless compositions and agonized over arithmetic. We took tests, sent them away to be corrected by faceless overseers in Baltimore, and eventually were promoted to the next grade level.

My mother was a demanding teacher with little patience for slow learners. Her new responsibility gave her a godlike status, far beyond any respect I'd felt for her before, that was coupled with a very real fear. She dominated every aspect of my life; the shadowed figure of my early childhood had been replaced by a woman who kept me spellbound and scared the hell out of me, whose approval I tried desperately to win.

Our home turned into a world of upstairs-downstairs, with the three oldest children working doggedly, lesson by lesson, on the second floor and my mother with her two youngest moving in blissful freedom below. She ruled our household; at some point my father began to flatten out, becoming an adjunct to the force that was my mother. Perhaps in response to that, he erupted into frequent tirades of rage, with an undercurrent that I didn't understand and didn't trust. He became easy to avoid and after years of following him wherever he went, I left him alone as much as I could.

Part Two
What She Gave

Four families going to Anchor Point on Election Day, 1960

Chapter Eleven

Alaska was a place where almost everybody grew up poor. Men made tiny fortunes fishing or working construction and then spent every cent of it to get through the winter. All of my friends grew up the way I did, and they were usually like me, the oldest in the family who shouldered more responsibility than any child would be allowed by law nowadays. We had to; we were needed. It made us feel grown up and important. That was our pay-off.

Every mother had the same work load as mine; few women had small families. Only children were pitiable in everyone's eyes because they had nobody to play with and never had to learn how to share. Families with two children were rarities; a little girl I knew once referred to them as "a rich man's family." Certainly two children siphoned off less income than five or six—or eight, which was the maximum number of offspring in our community. Our family of five children was average.

Billy and Martha's mother had the time to make diamond-shaped sandwiches with the crusts cut off. My mother slapped out pans of biscuits at lunchtime and served them hot, slathered with margarine and strawberry jam. She could make them with the speed of a factory worker, often impatiently pulling them out of the oven when they were still slightly too soft in the middle. Two pans of biscuits served all five of us, plus my father, for lunch, with a few as leftovers, and minimal dishwashing afterwards.

Efficiency was the keynote here, as it was for most of the meals that my mother prepared. The food she served had the same lackluster nourishment that characterized offerings in a school cafeteria, with lots of starch and little flavor. The cakes that she brought out for dessert were our rewards for chewing and swallowing potatoes or macaroni, bland in spite of the dried spices that she tossed in to give meals an exotic cast.

At the end of every summer, my parents would send an order to a wholesale grocery company and a month or so later my father would bring home the supplies that would get us through the winter. Fifty-pound bags of flour and sugar, a twenty-pound bag of salt, shortening in cans large enough to provide additional seating at the dinner table when company came, two-pound cans of ground coffee, ten-pound boxes of powdered milk, gallon glass jars of peanut butter and strawberry jam, and many cans of vegetables.

Canned fruit was a luxury for us, so was Jello, but my father, whose metabolism was high, bought penny candy in bulk for jolts of quick energy. Boxes of lollipops, licorice sticks, horehound drops, tootsie rolls, and jawbreakers enchanted our friends when they came over to play. "Your house is like living in a candy store," one of them breathed when invited to choose a lollipop from a box, but I knew better. One of my aunts in the states owned a candy store and what she had given us when we visited was confectionary that was often chocolate, not these hard, unyielding lumps of sugar and artificial flavorings. The candy that was stored away in our household was more akin to alcohol kept for medicinal purposes.

My parents kept no liquor in the house except for an occasional bottle of wine for holiday meals, but they were constantly wired on coffee. When I first learned to talk, one of my standard welcomes to guests was, "Come in sit down have a cup of coffee," delivered in one exuberant burst of air. Coffee was always steeping in the percolator, strong, hot, and bitter. Having no coffee in the pot was almost as bad as having no fire in the barrel stove. It meant disaster and one of the first things I ever learned to do in the kitchen was how to measure coffee into the percolator basket and carefully position it on the stem that was almost submerged in the pot of water. The sound of coffee perking was one of the most comforting sounds I knew. It meant that everyone within earshot was going to sit down and take a break and all chores were temporarily suspended

Fresh was an adjective reserved for impertinent children and was rarely applied to food. Fruit came in Christmas stockings, their toes heavy with an orange or apple that was mealy and tasteless, or in cans. Bananas were usually mottled, more brown than yellow, and often the deep black that meant banana bread would soon scent the house. Root vegetables were the only ones we ate that didn't require a can opener to prepare—potatoes, onions, turnips, and rutabagas.

Even the women who had gardens canned almost everything they grew. They processed fish, clams, and moose meat, turning protein into mush for the winter. They picked blueberries and cranberries to make jars of jam and jelly. To my mother, all that meant was a lot of labor for additional tedium at mealtime, along with the risk of botulism to spark things up a bit. Our canned goods came from a federally-regulated food facility, tomatoes, corn, spinach, and peas that had once been grown in warmer climates.

Much of the food that has now become chic and expensive was commonplace when I was growing up. Sushi, ceviche, steak tartare—I knew them long before I encountered them in a restaurant. When I was small, I ate the fragments of partially frozen meat when my father butchered a haunch of moose on the kitchen table. I ate raw clams on the way home after a morning of digging them up on the beach. And although my mother never canned anything, she learned how to pickle salmon, which retained a large amount of texture while adding a sour zing to the chunks of fish. Uncooked, it still had a hint of freshness when we ate it months after it had been caught.

In the summer, our meals were transformed by food that I can't afford now and often disdain when it comes my way. Little of the fish and seafood I've had as an adult compares to what I ate as a poor kid in Alaska—king salmon, fried razor clams, steamed butter clams, mussels, king crab, none of it frozen, all of it only a couple of hours away from having been alive.

One year a man who had been crossing the muskeg came to our house in a state of high excitement. He had just shot a bear. It was too early for the salmon run so my father knew the meat was probably edible, unlike the bear meat that he brought home to my mother early in their Alaskan years which had proved to taste like fish after it had been cooked. The neighbor only wanted the hide and my father brought home the butchered carcass. He hung it in a shed and built a fire from alder chunks, a slow-burning wood that smoked profusely. It was our job to keep that fire burning. If the flies got to it, the meat would be spoiled. What had recently been a bear looked horribly like the body of a man as it hung in its perpetual cloud of smoke. In the end, nobody wanted to eat it and my father gave it away to someone who fed it to his dog team.

Moose was the staple of our lives, shot out of season when money was dwindling, the world was frozen solid, and the meat would keep outdoors. It was usually the only food on our plates that required the use of molars, other than the ceremonial Thanksgiving turkey, and it was so lean that when we finally had beef, the fat coated our mouths and made us sick. "I want moose," one of my little sisters repeatedly begged during the winter we spent in Manhattan, and she cried when she was told that the beef on her plate was moose meat. We knew that difference; we were Alaskan children, carnivore connoisseurs of wild meat long before we ever went to school.

Chapter Twelve

My mother was a rager, not a whiner. One Thanksgiving Day when the butane stove ran out of fuel while the turkey was roasting, she wrapped the whole thing up, plopped it into a cardboard box and commandeered my sled. Together we took it half a mile down the hill to our nearest neighbor's cabin. They were spending the day in church so my mother calmly asserted squatter's rights to their stove for a few hours, finished the turkey, put it back on the sled, and carried it back up to our dinner table.

She made that an adventure, a small triumph, a story. Rising to the occasion was one of her major talents, and her new home provided her with many opportunities to do that over and over again. This was where she had always intended to be, in her own domain of wind, grass, and trees, not stuck as she had been for years in a little town where people gathered at the Community Club for potluck suppers and talked about the neighbors who didn't show up.

Now that she had a large house, she no longer pushed us out the door to play. She didn't have to. We went outside on our own accord, infected by my mother's contagious sense of adventure that had emerged with the move. We explored the groves of trees that were sprinkled through the miles of meadows and turned the closest one into a playground. We could make as much noise as we wanted; in fact we were encouraged to be loud when we were out in the woods. "Yell, sing, fight—it keeps the bears away," my father said.

Part Two
What She Gave

The wind was constant. There were days when we knew we could turn into kites and soar, running down the hill in front of our house, feeling the gusts push us along, waiting for the one that would catch us and send us into flight. My father made kites from newspapers and bits of lath, making us help him in the painstaking, tedious work that could be demolished in a few minutes or captured in a surge of air, never to be seen again.

I couldn't see the point to flying kites. He handed me the string to one that was successfully soaring one day, to keep it safe while he had a cup of coffee. Bored, I had found a book and accepted the kite string without looking up, lost in the story. When the kite gave an especially peremptory tug, without thinking I let it go, not noticing its absence until my father came back to reclaim it. He went into a mammoth sulk and my sisters congratulated me after he stamped back inside to his coffee. We all hated those damned kites.

The igloo was much more of a hit, although at first we had our doubts about it. We had been rolling giant snowballs to make a fort, packing the spaces between the rock-solid globes with loose snow, when my father emerged from the house and began to construct snow bricks. It took hours but by the end of the day, with our help, he had constructed a perfect igloo. It was large enough to stand up in and when we did, we were surrounded by pale blue light. It was too cold to spend much time within its solid, curving walls, but it looked very pretty and it was enduring. Long after the snow around it had melted in the spring, the igloo still stood, slowly shrinking until all that remained was a small circle of icy, dirty snow.

There were days when storms blew in, dashing rain against the windows and tossing the branches of the two large spruce trees that stood near the house so violently that even indoors we could hear them creaking. Sometimes we'd wake up surrounded by a fog thick enough to hide everything outside our windows and for a few hours we would be marooned on our own desert island.

I think my mother saw us as a modern day Swiss Family Robinson, resourceful, adventurous, and self-sufficient. What we truly became were anachronisms. While she and my father had other reference points, for us our homestead was the whole world. We'd study the pages of the Sears catalog, looking at the weird magic of a TV set, a fully-stocked refrigerator, or a mower traveling across a tidy green lawn. What we saw was as unreal to us as the bright and sterile stories of Dick, Jane, and Sally in the silly books we'd been given to read in the Anchor Point school.

We were little girls who lived in sweatshirts and blue jeans, ran barefoot when it turned warm until the first snowfall forced us to put on small versions of my father's shoepacks, hurtled down hills on sleds in the winter and rode horseback in the summer, shrieked our lungs out the minute we stepped outside. We were what my mother wanted us to be. Unfortunately the vision she had for us when we grew up was completely incongruous to what we were encouraged to become in childhood. Wild girls don't magically become sedate Ivy League co-eds upon command. But then none of the girls I grew up with became the adults that their parents wished them to be.

View from our house on the hill, with miniature haystack

Part Two
What She Gave

Kachemak Bay, near Homer

Light and Silence

Chapter Thirteen

My father would go out into the world, visit friends, talk, and find treasures to bring home. That was how the horses came into our lives, and soon after that he found an electric generator in a household that lived near newly planted power poles. It was a gigantic monster that had to be started with a mammoth hand crank and looked as though it was a remnant of the Industrial Revolution.

A twisted ganglia of electric wire and sockets filled our house. Eventually one evening my father cranked up the generator and we had lights and music on a functioning record player. The monster had brought us back to a semblance of 20th century comfort but it was a moody, capricious apparatus that could die without warning, in the middle of a sonata. Submerged in sudden darkness, my parents would scramble for flashlights and light the Blazo lanterns.

When the generator chugged and produced light, we spread out over the house but when the lanterns were lit, we huddled together in one spot, always reading. Beneath their glass coverings, the cloth mantles threw out a clear white light but it didn't travel well so we crammed together, as close to the lanterns as we could get.

There was never enough to read. We fought over who would be the first to read *Life* or *The Saturday Evening Post*, after my parents had finished with them. The *Post* had cartoons and *Life* was all photos, a television set bound in paper. Some of the best photojournalists in the world published their work on the pages of *Life* and it was always a wonderful surprise to see what they had to show us every week.

By the time I was ten, I knew about Balenciaga, Princess Luciana Pignatelli, winter sports at St Moritz, and bikinis on the Riviera. I saw the dark and horrible consequences of mercury poisoning and the incomprehensible cruelty of Little Rock. Renata Tebaldi, Sophia Loren, Richard Nixon, Robert Frost, the Shah of Iran, the beautiful flower-faced Queen of Thailand—I studied these images and imagined their lives beyond what was given to me in a few photographs and a paragraph or two of snappy prose.

Earlier, when at six I was already a gluttonous reader, a box arrived near my birthday and I was allowed to open it. Inside were the six most popular novels of Louisa May Alcott, bright, shiny, and new—all for me. I read them and reread them over the next nine years, until their cheap bindings had disintegrated and the pages were loose-leaf. Long after their glossy, colored dust jackets were tattered and thrown away, those books were my treasures, my personal library.

Alaska had one bookstore then, the Book Cache in Anchorage, and my parents bought paperbacks there every time they were in town. Their purchases were all classics and philosophy; since my father had left school at fourteen when the Depression hit, he was a life-long autodidact. He may be the only person I ever met who read every volume of the Encyclopedia Britannica that a salesman persuaded my mother to buy in installment payments one summer.

Snack reading came in boxes of paperbacks that were passed from household to household in Anchor Point and made their way to us even after we moved away. Most of those books were pulp fiction with garish covers and yellowing pages, the cheap glue that bound them together already cracked and useless and the paper exuding the smell of wet wood, but there were unexpected gems among them. Picking through the cardboard cartons when they arrived, choosing the books we wanted to read, was a big event in our house, almost as much fun as the monthly library boxes.

Alaska sent cartons of books into the wilds by mail. Everybody in a family could tick off what they liked to read when they signed up for this service, and librarians in the state capital of Juneau would choose books that would correspond as closely as possible to the tastes of each individual reader. What was in the carton was always a surprise and we looked forward to this as though Christmas came every month.

Then the Anchor Point Community Club decided the town needed a library of its very own. They found space in an abandoned one-room schoolhouse and men filled it with bookshelves made of rough lumber. Two women volunteered to keep the library open one day a week and they requested assistance from Juneau. They were told if they could come up with a core collection of one hundred cloth-bound books as the genesis of the library, along with a group of people who would borrow them regularly, they would become an official institution with books provided by the state of Alaska.

Finding one hundred books in a community of ninety-eight people was a mammoth task. Books were either hard-bound treasures or ephemeral paperbacks. Nobody had the money to buy a new book to donate to something that might not ever come to fruition. And it probably wouldn't have, if it hadn't been for a man with a reverence for books who had once been a garbage man in Anchorage. Every time he found a hard-cover book in somebody's trash, he brought it home. By the time he retired, his collection was both motley and expansive. That became the nucleus of our library.

Once it opened, every week I would ride my horse on a twenty-mile round trip with two burlap bags filled with the maximum number of volumes that my family could borrow—sixteen books. When a storm blew in, I would spend the night at the house of a family friend. Otherwise I could make it to town and back in one day.

It was always special to go to the library and enter that room full of books, even though many of them were so old and battered that they were almost unreadable. When books began to arrive from Juneau, they were displayed with pride. Their shiny covers protected with plastic gleamed among the shelves of unjacketed books. The highest accolade the librarian knew how to give as she showed us new additions to her collection was, "Look. It's a brand new book."

House on the hill

Chapter Fourteen

My mother had no privacy for most of her life, unless she escaped into a book or behind the wheel of her car. Someone was always calling her, a child, her husband. She was the center of our lives and we needed her.

Perhaps once a year she would announce that she was going to take a walk, taking nobody with her but the dogs, alone in the solitude and beauty that she looked at through her windows every day. And only once did she ever tell me to saddle one of the horses for her, on a long blue summer evening when she rode off to look for my father, who was late in coming home from town.

She loved where she lived, she loved the horses. She never rode, she rarely walked through the woods alone. Instead she watched us as we did all of that for her.

Much of my mother's stern vigilance over us faded away when we left Anchor Point. She had her own social realm back in the hills and she made her own rules. Table manners were the keystone of her dictatorship, followed by exhortations that demanded no interruptions and no whining. No talking back was a slippery slope for all of us because there was a thin line between independent thinking and the flouting of authority. Both of my parents appreciated a good argument, even if it came from one of their children, and they regarded sarcasm as an art form.

We lived in rough country that demanded a lot from those who wanted to be part of it. Visiting was the primary form of recreation for people who had no television, no movie theaters, no coffee shops. The trail used by other homesteaders went right past our house for years, and the sound of approaching motors floated up the hill long before any vehicle showed itself. That gave us time to put on a fresh pot of coffee and our company manners, while we waited to see who was coming.

It was unthinkable not to greet whoever it might be and ask them in for a warm-up; it would be unspeakable to refuse the invitation. I remember only one time when a passing neighbor didn't stop. He called out bad news about a car accident, a dead boy, an injured girl, and kept on going. In a community that didn't put on black when mourning was called for, this was the way we paid respect to the dead.

Anyone who passed our house became an instant guest, whether we knew them or not. Once a man appeared over the crest of the hill, a dark shape emerging from a snowstorm, silhouetted in our front windows. He knocked on the door, asking directions to land he wanted to claim under the Homestead Act. He stayed with us for three months until break-up, when the world thawed out, and became one of my father's best friends.

My father was the genial host; my mother was more reserved. She listened more than she spoke. My father did the talking; my mother did the analyzing. Always polite, sometimes very funny with a sharp jab of wit, she was the one whose good opinion was valued.

She got away with bloody murder in a town where domestic tasks dominated most of the other women's time. She hated to keep house, so she didn't. Only because of who she was did she fail to become the town pariah. This, the other women decided, was just who Jan was. She was special; she was smart; she was a New Yorker with important things on her mind.

My mother politely refused when she was approached with the magnanimous offer to become president of the Women's Club, if she would only join. She laughed about it later when she told me, but her disclosure horrified me.

"Why didn't you do it?" I asked, in an accent that was largely Pacific Northwestern, pronunciation that made my mother correct me every time I opened my mouth. Her accent was still East Coast born and bred to the very core and her attitude toward any kind of club was engrained. Her own mother had left the D.A.R. when they prevented Marian Anderson from singing in Washington DC.

I was hybrid; what was taking hold in me were the hard r's and flat vowels of the people I heard every day. I said tomahto instead of tahmaytah but crick instead of creek and parky for parka. I would have loved it if my mother had chosen to be president of the Women's Club but as I grew older I realized my mother's leadership in our community was both more subtle and more powerful.

Family Portrait, 1953

Part Two
What She Gave

Barefoot in the summer, 1954

Light and Silence

Chapter Fifteen

At the end of her life, my mother's voice floated thin and cracked as it came to me over the phone. She told me about the dream she had in which she was writing a book. "What was it about?" I asked and she replied tersely, "How to be the perfect house guest."

In Alaska nobody could afford the extravagance of a hotel room and when my mother went to Anchorage, she stayed with friends. Being a house guest was not an unknown talent for which she had been given no preparation. Now confined to a bed in a room in someone else's home, every minute that she was awake, she probably worried about her television or her CD player being too loud. I'm sure she fretted over not cleaning her plate when her meals were brought to her. I know that being touched by strangers was only bearable because it was better than the intimacy of being bathed and dressed by one of her daughters.

And yet she would never complain about this. That wasn't in my mother's code of behavior.

My grandmother said to me once when talking about my mother, "And there never was a kick out of her." Of course there were no letters either. Year after year, as soon as I could hold a pen, my grandmother and I wrote each other letters. Hers always contained a dollar, for us all to share, and ended with "How is your mother?"

My mother had been left some land in Maine as an inheritance, when she was still young enough that it had to be put in my grandmother's name. When one of her nephews came with a real estate scheme that involved her daughter's acreage, my grandmother sold it to him. My mother never forgave her.

My grandmother came to Alaska when I was little, when my father was working at what is now called Denali National Park. She saw how my mother lived and she was properly horrified. One day when she was taking care of my sister and me, she saw a bear come into the front yard and begin to nose around the door of our house, looking for garbage. When my parents came home, they couldn't get inside until my grandmother had pulled away the large chest of drawers she had managed to push against the door. Wilderness living held no charms for her and she soon returned to her city apartment. I'm positive she did her best to persuade her daughter to come back too, without any hope of success.

We went to New York for an entire winter when I turned six. We lived in a tenement building in Yorkville, the same slum neighborhood that I had been born in, near Jacob Ruppert's brewery. I had my first library card, my sisters and I were taken to play in Central Park every day, and went ceremoniously to my grandmother's tiny apartment every Sunday evening to watch television. When Easter approached, my mother had the money, probably given by one of her brothers, to buy us spring outfits from Macy's and in my little pink coat and hat with its sprig of cloth violets and long streamers of pink ribbon, I owned New York.

When our parents slept late on weekend mornings, my sisters and I entertained ourselves by peering through our bathroom window into the window of the apartment across the airshaft. We called it watching television and knew it was a clandestine pleasure; it ended when a man saw my little sister's face staring at him. He shook his fist at her and pulled down the blinds.

We were forbidden to leave the apartment alone but my sister and I did, only once. My parents were in a raging battle that showed no signs of abating. We huddled in the bedroom whose empty doorway led directly into the combat zone. There was no escaping the screams, the curses, the bitter words, the thud of hurled ashtrays. "Let's go to Gammy's," I whispered and my sister stopped crying.

I was positive I knew the way from East 92nd to my grandmother's apartment on East 35th Street; I was a native New Yorker. We tiptoed to the living room door and walked through it, closing it softly behind us as we reached the hallway. Then we ran to the elevator and went down to the entrance of our building. The street beyond was full of old people sitting on the stoops of the shabby brownstones, monitoring the neighborhood, and one of them was someone who knew us.

He lived in our building; when he discovered we had no grandfather, he had volunteered for the job. Seeing our determined little faces, tear-stained and grim with purpose, he immediately stepped in.

"What are you doing outside without your parents?" he asked. We were too young to make up a convincing story, so we told him the truth. "Let me take you back home," he said and we shook our heads. "Will you go home if I give you both a banana?"

He led us upstairs to our door and watched as we slipped back inside. Our parents were still locked in battle; they never noticed that we had gone, or had come back.

Soon after that, one of my uncles gave his sister her first car, a maroon Studebaker sedan. We all fit ourselves into it and began the long camping trip back home to Alaska.

Part Two
What She Gave

The hills that my mother loved

Light and Silence

Chapter Sixteen

It was a dismal, grey, wet afternoon, the kind that lingered for months in Anchor Point, when my mother told me to put on my slicker, boots, and rain hat and handed me a worn and crumpled piece of paper. "It's a treasure map that I found in a book," she told me, "Go outside and see where it takes you."

I was five and the directions were simple ones, but there were many of them. "Walk to the clover hill. Turn right. Walk to the first dead tree that you can see and turn left." Following the terse sentences, I walked around the area outside our house for at least an hour. The final order was to walk to the site of our last bonfire, pick up a shovel, and dig near the biggest partially burned log. There buried in the soft ashes was a small cloth bag that held a handful of marbles, with two that were almost translucent: an emerald, a ruby, treasure that was now mine.

When my mother wasn't tired or depressed, that sort of ingenuity and imagination was what she brought to our lives. Our birthday parties were always festive and the honored child could do whatever she wanted on that day. She concocted basic costumes for us on Halloween; one October she reddened the lips and darkened the eyebrows on my little brother's face, draped him in some gauzy fabric and sent him out with us as our visiting Siamese cousin. My brother was only two and was a bit confused by the gender switch until he discovered that candy was involved. He seemed honestly disappointed when he went back to his normal, less exotic state, consoled only by his well-supplied trick or treat bag.

Part Two
What She Gave

My youngest and final sister was a good tempered baby who early on was quick to see the jokes in life. Like any Alaskan child, she became enchanted by sunlight and when she waved her hands, playing with their shadows, my mother told us she was talking to the beams of light, that they contained little people that only my sister could see. And this may have been true; as soon as she could talk, my baby sister turned out to have a whole family of friends that were invisible to all but her.

Imagination was what kept us all amused and when my mother entered that world with us, it became sanctioned in a lawless fashion. The day that we burst into the house with some friends to have our lunch and were greeted by a woman who looked exactly like our mother but who told us she was a witch named Agatha was one that opened up fascinating possibilities. If nothing else, the sheer joyful anarchy of being on a first-name basis with a woman whose persona was usually the stern daughter of the voice of God had us all spellbound. From then on, when my mother was in a good mood, I'd come into the kitchen inquiring tentatively "Agatha?" and was delighted when she would respond.

Her humor was dry and it often cut to the bone as I got older. When I hit the 8th grade and "graduation" loomed, my friends and I were deeply immersed in discussions over what we should wear to the ceremony. Someone brought a Sears catalog to school and we made our selections. Mine was a black, one-shouldered sheath dress worn by a model who was a watered-down version of Liz Taylor. I knew I could carry that off and all of my friends agreed with me. Their own choices involved décolletage and pastels but my dress, they assured me, was "sophisticated."

My mother's reaction was one of barely restrained hysterical laughter when I told her what I wanted for my emergence into the world of adolescence, and her own suggestion was vastly more practical. It wouldn't have been so bad if she hadn't made it in public, at the post office, in front of the mothers of many of my friends. "We should get each of the girls a muu-muu," she announced, "it will work for everybody—the fat ones, the skinny ones, the ones who don't yet have a bust."

I didn't get the joke, but the other mothers did, and some of my friends didn't speak to me for days. But it did make my pink shirtwaist graduation dress seem quite acceptable when I considered the Waikiki beach alternative that could have been mine.

Cook Inlet beach in Anchor Point, with Mount Iliamna

Part Two
What She Gave

Kachemak Bay, always photogenic

Chapter Seventeen

The cliché "You can't choose your family but you can choose your friends" wasn't true in Alaskan small towns. Those communities were strangely intertwined organisms made up of people who had one thing in common. They had to accept each other because they all needed each other.

If a car went into the ditch, any passing neighbor would stop to help push it back on the road. If a house burned down, people who had very little shared what they had with the family who lost everything. If a woman needed medical care, her offspring went to stay with another family. If a man needed a tool that he didn't possess, he could borrow it from someone who did. It was a lot like Aldous Huxley's *Island* without the Utopia.

My father was a gregarious man and he rapidly adjusted to this. My mother was bred from centuries of Maine reserve and she did not. When her house was lost in a flaming conflagration and each of her three little daughters went to stay with separate families; when she returned with her burned arms that had been treated but weren't yet healed to a small one-room cabin that one of the bachelors had lent us to stay in for the rest of the winter; when the room became filled with cardboard cartons that had been left on our doorstep, stuffed with everything from clothing to kitchen utensils to dolls, she withdrew. She lived in a little cocoon of loss, pain, and pride for a long time.

I was four and to me the boxes were all wonderful presents. I burrowed through them gleefully as my mother sat in silence and tried to fade away.

Part Two
What She Gave

I learned not to care that she was present but not with me. I had another family to retreat to, a houseful of little girls.

I had stayed with this family from the time I was two and after my first stint with them I came home speaking Finn. Thelma and Arnie were both from Finland and if I wanted someone to pass me the butter at their table, they insisted I learn to ask in their language. They owned Anchor Point's only café and they were rarely home, except for an occasional meal. The household was run by the eldest of their five daughters, who was probably twelve when I first became one of the girls.

Their house was in a large meadow that was a short distance from the shores of Cook Inlet and our playground was the beach. The older girls had work to do; the chores of the youngest were minimal—and since I was one of the youngest, the time I spent in that house was filled with finding shells and Japanese green glass floats on the beach, or sitting in the upstairs bedroom playing with paper dolls that we cut out from old Sears catalogs, eating freshly baked cookies. At night we younger children huddled together in a big bed and Ellen, who was eight, whispered stories until we all fell asleep.

It was my favorite place to be. When my mother came home with her first new baby, I returned from my other family, inspected my sister, pronounced her very nice, turned to my father and asked, "Will you please take me back to Thelma and Arnie's house now?"

There was never a question of whether I liked the house full of girls or if they liked me. We were all part of the same family. So was my friend Johnny, who stayed with us once in a while, or Gary, who lived nearby and whose proposal of marriage I turned down when I was four. And after the fire, when we moved to the house my father built for us in the middle of Anchor Point, my mother learned how to know the mothers of the children I was close to, in her own way—with her mixture of kindness and distance.

Thelma was a woman who worked outside of her home, which made her a sought-after cook when people could afford to eat at her café, as well as an anomaly in 1950's Anchor Point. Johnny's mother was a delightful essence of pure tomboy with a beautiful smile. She and her husband Lefty always seemed like twins to me. Gary's mother Vi was a deeply religious Pentecostal who grieved that my mother's Catholic soul was doomed to hellfire. Her mournful personality was balanced by the enticing fact that she made doughnuts and maple bars which she occasionally gave to us when we went to her house to play. My mother learned to respect these women, and like them too, but she had little to discuss with them besides their children.

In many ways she had more in common with me. Like her, by the time I was four I was a greedy reader with a dazzling memory and a parroted vocabulary. I was Anchor Point's *wunderkind*; people used to come to our house to hear me read the newspaper long before I lost my first baby tooth. I would have been an obnoxious, pompous little brat if I hadn't met Patty when I first went to school.

Patty could do everything well. She read as much as I did, she drew beautifully, and she was a whiz at kickball. She too had a New York grandmother, but hers worked at Best & Company and sent Patty beautiful clothes from Manhattan. Her mother often set her hair in fat and perfect ringlets, but this girl was no candy-box princess. Patty ran fast, climbed high, and was absolutely fearless. Her imagination was as vivid as mine, and although I was a year younger, we became close friends.

Our games were imaginary dramas that we concocted from a single sentence; sometimes we could get the entire schoolyard involved in one for days. We were savage readers and often sat side by side reading companionably. Visiting Patty was wonderful because together we did everything I would do if I were alone.

Her mother had been a ballet dancer in New York; a framed black and white photo of her wearing a tutu and slippers hung on the wall of their cabin. Dottie was lean and fierce and very funny, specializing in the dry sarcasm that my mother shared and loved. They were both exceedingly private and would probably have never met if Patty and I hadn't become friends. Yet they did and liked each other immediately—two Manhattan girls with brains and energy who knew that Alaska was where they wanted

Part Two
What She Gave

to raise their children.

Dottie and my mother were never as close as Patty and I were, but they were two women with a common language. Nobody can be quite as provincial as a New Yorker. Different neighborhoods are different worlds and these women came from backgrounds that were gapingly dissimilar, but they had shared passions. Their infrequent visits must have been both nourishing and painful, since each of them was certainly at times profoundly homesick for the city that had shaped them. Yet finally, after years of isolation, my mother knew another woman who also loved ballet, music, books—and Alaska. Each of them watched their children grow into people they would never have become had they grown up in Manhattan. Patty and I, each in our own way small blazing comets, burned hard and fast. We never became the stars our mothers planned for us to be.

Over half a century from the time that Patty and I collided in a one-room school, we no longer write the long, news-filled letters that linked us when we were parted in childhood. We haven't seen each other in almost forty years. But our mothers wrote each other notes, and visited occasionally, still rattling off stories to each other with East Coast speed, still making their sardonic little jokes, still laughing. They were among the few survivors of Anchor Point women from the 1950s—still at their cores stylish New Yorkers with eccentric dreams.

Chapter Eighteen

I grew up in a land without telephones. If my mother needed help from one of her neighbors she'd dash off a quick handwritten note and I'd deliver it. Otherwise news came face-to-face or over the radio.

Radios were our links to the world, the way smart phones are now. Everybody had one and they were impressive pieces of furniture, often standing as tall as a night stand, encased in polished wood. The dials and tuner looked as though they were capable of navigating a small plane, often producing noises that sounded as though they came from outer space, high-pitched gurgling noises that emerged in a broken staccato. The internal workings were large glass tubes that appeared to contain liquid and I was certain that a tiny alchemist lived somewhere inside, working the magic that brought voices and music into our cabin.

It was unreliable magic. Sometimes it was impossible to get a broadcast from Anchorage but the BBC would come in loud and clear, with peals from Big Ben announcing the time. Or a voice would announce "This is Radio Moscow." Occasionally voices from fishing boats crackled into our living room, once in a while speaking Japanese. But when all worked as it should, the reassuring and neighborly sounds of radio stations broadcasting from Anchorage connected us to a more familiar world.

The announcers were cheery and personable. Their audience knew them by name and often heard them joking on the air with the broadcast crew. When the popular ones moved on, it was like losing a close friend—and that's what the announcer had become. He was there over morning coffee; he was sometimes the last voice heard at night. Especially for people like my mother, who spent months in a cabin without her husband, or for the bachelors who lived alone, the radio and its announcers were lifelines to a distant world.

Before I started school, there was a radio program in Anchorage that did live interviews with children who visited the broadcasting station. When I visited and said I had a dog named Nushnik, which meant outhouse in Russian, children who still spoke smatterings of Russian in villages once populated by Russian fur trappers collapsed in gleeful horror in front of their radios. Apparently our dog's name wasn't the most refined term for outdoor privy.

View of Iliamna from our homestead in the hills

At night, right around suppertime, a dead silence fell over our house while my parents listened to the world news. No child was allowed to make a sound while events were announced for a length of time that always seemed interminable. But when that was over, even we would cluster next to the radio. It was time for Mukluk Telegraph.

This was a public service offered by radio station KENI and it was the most popular time slot in Alaska. Deaths, births, homecomings, requests were all broadcast in personal messages in our world without telephones.

We never knew what familiar names would drift out of the radio at that time of night. If it was someone in Anchor Point, we made sure that they had heard the message. Who knew? Perhaps their radio wasn't working that evening.

Sometimes it was our own names that we heard, "Bill from Anchor Point wants Jan and the girls to know that he's coming home tomorrow at 7 pm on PNA." "The family and friends of Bill and Jan from Anchor Point will be happy to know that Jan had a little boy. Mother and baby are doing fine."

Nome, Allakaket, Tatalina, Nenana—we were all neighbors, linked by Mukluk Telegraph. Not a baby was born, not a death occurred anywhere in Alaska without it being announced on this program. In a territory that would soon become a state that was much bigger than Texas, with a population that wouldn't fill a small city anywhere else in the nation, Mukluk Telegraph brought us all together, sitting near our radios at the same time every night to get the news that mattered most.

One evening as we waited for my father to come home from town, a strange sound floated toward us in the darkness, coming up the hill and along the trail toward our house. As it grew louder and more distinct, we ran to meet the figure who approached us, wondering how it was possible that he walked in a cloud of music.

In my father's hands, he held the handle of a small black and silver box. Grinning, he came to my mother's side and handed her the box, the music. "I brought you a present, Jannie," he told her.

He turned to us. "It's a transistor radio, kids. It runs on flashlight batteries, it will play anywhere you want to put it. It's portable."

That night, long after we went to bed, music, clear and without static, moved to different rooms of our house. For years we had looked at pictures of modern appliances, televisions, refrigerators, washer/dryer combos, all as unattainable to Alaskan homesteaders as year-round sunlight. Now at last, a tiny piece of the outside world belonged to us.

Light and Silence

Chapter Nineteen

My father was a man who always had good ideas and at times they were even brilliant. As an oilfield worker, he organized his colleagues in a union effort that brought them into the International Brotherhood of Petroleum Workers.

That was a somewhat hazardous enterprise. The head of Alaska's Laborer's Union, dressed in a camel's hair overcoat and shiny black leather loafers, drove two hundred miles from Anchorage to our one-room cabin in Soldotna. My father was close to success and one of the state's most powerful unions was ready to step in and harvest a group of workers that they had previously ignored.

The discussion lasted hours, with all of us banished from the cabin until it was over. I'm sure there were generous offers and probably a couple of veiled threats, but my father refused to hand over his co-workers. At this stage of my life, I didn't like my father very much but I was smart enough to realize that what he was doing was admirable and honorable. He didn't sell out.

But long before this, when we were small, his ideas frequently evoked nothing but our hearty disapproval. They were creative but often went way beyond the scope of reality. We howled our dissent when he offered to build a barn so our cats no longer had to live in the house with us and when he suggested that we get one big "family" present for Christmas, a set of electric trains, that plan was thoroughly repudiated by his little daughters.

Part Two
What She Gave

The winter that my mother had hepatitis and went to New York, my father's creativity had no barriers. "We'll have a cocoa spring that will never go dry. You'll drink cocoa whenever you want it," he promised and mixed cocoa, powdered milk, sugar, and water in a brand new two and a half gallon metal bucket. This went on the top of the barrel stove and stayed there for five months, replenished with ingredients, never emptied.

"It's silly to spend too much time in the kitchen. We're going to be efficient," he said. The results of this pronouncement were bizarre. Sometimes he'd make a huge batch of cinnamon rolls which we ate for days. A basinful of rice pudding was another staple. "It's nourishing," he told us, "look, I'm making it with eggs, milk, and rice—it's good for you." Hasty pudding, made with cornmeal, was a dismal failure, which he found difficult to understand. "It's what the pioneers ate; the Indians taught them how to make it. You're eating history," he insisted. We gagged and when his back was turned, we fed it to the dogs.

With our confidence shaken, we rebelled. "We want real food," we demanded, "We want supper, not dessert for supper." My father pouted for a while and then announced that we were absolutely right. "Tonight," he assured us, "We'll have chicken noodle soup, but you'll all have to help me make it."

This was a masterstroke that turned small mutineers back into co-conspirators. For us, true children of our time and place, chicken noodle soup came in only one form. It was yellow, salty broth, with small, flavorless squares of chicken and short, thin, squishy noodles. It came in a red and white can. It was supreme comfort food, always eaten with saltines, and it never occurred to our limited points of view that it could take on any other guise than that.

Tossing a couple of spruce hens into a large pot with half a dozen yellow onions, salt, pepper, and a gallon of water, my father announced jubilantly that this would be our soup. Still credulous, we inquired about the noodles. "We're going to make them," my father replied, "go and get all of the coat hangers you can find."

Light and Silence

We watched him make dough, roll it out, and cut it into thick strips. "These," he told us with a note of triumph in his voice, "are the noodles."

"They don't look like noodles," my smallest sister observed tremulously and the rest of us agreed, even my little brother, who could barely talk.

"Just wait," my father promised, "They have to dry before they're done."

All of us draped ribbons of dough over wire coat hangers and my father hung them from the ceiling. For the rest of the day, we dodged dangling strips of something we were positive we didn't want to eat.

We watched the dough hit the boiling water that the spruce hens had simmered in for most of the day. Bits of skin and bone roiled about with chunks of onions and wet, unbaked bread. When at last it was ladled into bowls, we tasted it, hoping for a miracle. Then the uprising hit full force.

"It's not chicken noodle soup. This is disgusting," I protested, knowing that it was my responsibility as the oldest to speak up. "I can't eat this. It's going to make me sick." The others murmured their assent, tears welling up in their eyes.

"I want Mommy," my little brother sobbed and we all began to cry. My father knew when he was defeated. "Let's have toast and peanut butter for supper tonight," he suggested. The soup went to the dogs.

Then came the day that we were invited to have supper with friends in town, an event we all looked forward to. A few days before this occasion, my father looked dubiously at our winter coats. "They're very dirty," he decided.

"Yes," I agreed, "but they're wool. Mommy says they can't go in the washing machine because they'll shrink. They have to go to a dry cleaner." I had no idea what a dry cleaner was, but my father seemed to understand.

"Let me think about this," he said and went off to the corner of the couch with his cigarette and cup of coffee. My father smoked a lot; he said it helped him figure things out.

My sisters and I looked at each other with a generous helping of apprehension and then went off to play. Whatever he thought up, at least it wouldn't involve something we would have to eat.

Within a couple of hours, he called for us to bring our coats outside. When we came to where he stood, we all began to cough. My father was standing beside a large washtub that was filled with Blazo. Even in the sharp winter air, the fumes were intense.

"Give me your coats," he said and plunged them into the Blazo. "This is dry cleaning. The gas will clean the wool in a couple of hours, without our having to lift a finger. Some people pay to have this done," he scoffed.

We had to admit the coats were much cleaner when eventually they emerged from their immersion in white gas. Once again the coat hangers came into play; our coats were so permeated with fumes that we couldn't bring them in the house. They hung outside on the clothesline for the next two days.

Even so, we still smelled strongly of Blazo when we put them on for our social engagement. "You look very nice," my father said approvingly, "but of course you're going to have to ride in the back of the pickup truck."

It was a beautiful day, crisp, clear, and blindingly white and blue. We sang all the way into town, in our clean winter coats, peering into the cab where my father drove with one hand. The other held the reason we were in the back, his perpetual cigarette, its tip glowing with a subdued flame.

Chapter Twenty

Mid-century rural Alaskan women had no time or money to spend on clothes, My mother often left her house wearing a sweatshirt, blue jeans, one of my father's army surplus parkas, and a pair of warm and sturdy boots, with a plaid woolen headscarf tied babushka-fashion over her hair.

The total effect was very Soviet. When we spent one winter in a small town with a little supermarket a mile from our cabin, my mother would hop on the Ford tractor, drive it to the store, fill the rumble seat with groceries, and drive back home. In her scarf and army parka, perched upon her tractor, driving through the snow, she looked like a photograph from a *National Geographic* feature on indomitable Russian women. But when she walked through that grocery store, she always carried herself as though she were shopping on Fifth Avenue.

When I was growing up, I silently mocked my mother's gift for self-delusion. The truth was she simply didn't care what other people thought of her. That most of the other women around her dressed the same way must have helped her lack of embarrassment. Alaska was filled with eccentrics and my mother was widely admired in her little community for having the resourcefulness to use a tractor as the family's second car. Decades later when I met someone from Kenai, "Your mother was the one who used to get around town on a tractor" would usually enter the conversation and always in tones of admiration.

She was more akin to a young version of one of Nancy Mitford's dowager duchesses than to Holy Mother Russia. Her disregard of public opinion was inbred by centuries of New England rectitude and it drove her wild when I began to study fashion magazines, looking for trends to follow. She wanted me to become the well-scrubbed future debutante with a shiny pageboy that she had once been, but my fashion role model became Anita in *West Side Story*.

My mother should have realized that you don't get a debutante from a little girl who was taught to admire pirates and gypsies. Finishing school manners go only surface-deep when a child spends most of her time outdoors, roaming for miles in forests and open grassland. Where I lived was the perfect Petri dish for raising a rebel and for years nothing was done to discourage that tendency in me. I think at heart my mother truthfully liked that I was becoming the child's answer to the Noble Savage. Whether she admitted it to herself or not, she was carefully cultivating a human weapon of mass destruction, sarcastic, undisciplined, and a smartass.

There were personality quirks that arose in me as I approached adolescence that I'm sure I channeled straight from my mother. I was the child who didn't come in a set, as my two younger sisters and the two babies of the family did, and I was ruthless in my desire to be distant from the other children. "Privacy, I want privacy," I would howl at them and climbed a long ladder, book tucked under one arm, so I could read on the roof, two and a half stories above the convivial noise of our household. My mother never stopped me; my yearning for silence and uninterrupted reading mirrored her own

That same longing for solitude, coupled with the years of being sternly told to go outside and play, turned me into a child who was as comfortable outdoors as I was in a house. When we lived within walking distance of the shores of Cook Inlet, and walking distance was anything under five miles, I'd make a sandwich and set off for the long stretch of wind-scoured sand that we called "the beach." I learned to love it in winter even more than I did in summer, when rocks that stood higher than I were covered with a thick glaze of ice, and everywhere I looked, sand, sky, water, trees were all the same relentless shade of grey. Piles of driftwood made fine shelters against the stiff breeze that kicked up a wall of small but intense surf and I'd sit there to eat my sandwich and warm up a little before walking on and on, alone except for our dogs.

I learned to be comfortable with silence and space, whether I moved through it on foot or on horseback. When I came home, my mother never asked me where I went. She knew. I was enjoying the freedom she had given me, the gift of doing what she had always wanted.

She taught me to be fearless within the world that was ours. There were black bear and there were moose but I never saw them in my hours of walking through tall grass.

They preferred the muskeg, the bogs that stretched below the hills, with wallows of water, malformed, spindly trees, and bumper crops of wild berries. I loved the miles of meadowgrass, alive under the wind, stretching off into more and more hills where nobody lived. I never was tired of taking off with one of our dogs on one of the rare days that wasn't wet, finding old hunting trails to walk on, or pushing my way through unending waves of green.

On the hill we called ours, the sky was a key element of the landscape; weather blew in from the inlet, across the muskeg, pushing thick billows of mist in our direction. Clouds in peculiar shapes raced beyond our windows or settled in clumps of grey, thin and tattered, bringing rain.

On clear nights, especially in winter, stars glittered over the sculpted snowdrifts. The moon turned the grove of trees behind our house into a place that was unknown and unexplored, holding something that enticed me to come close and then made me turn back. On nights like that, we'd go sledding along the dunes of snow that took on a soft pearl-like glow in the moonlight.

My mother often told me of how she and my father crossed the border into Canada on their first drive to Alaska and immediately had their rifles sealed by the customs officers. If they left the country with those seals broken, the penalty would be severe. So they camped their way across Canada, along the Alcan highway that was at that time one of the least traveled on earth.

Part Two
What She Gave

They slept in a tent with their baby daughter, holding no defense against marauding animals—and they encountered none.

By the time they crossed the line that separated the Yukon Territory and Alaska, my mother had lost any vestigial urban fear that she might have brought with her from Manhattan, and she brought up her children to feel disdain for anybody who carried a gun for protection. We shared our country with animals that had been there long before we showed up and, we were assured, they were nothing to be afraid of.

When we lived in Kenai, the small town with the supermarket, I joined a Brownie troop that met after school once a week. When I walked to the church where the meetings took place, I was joined by quite a few sled dogs that were allowed to roam free, and they always accompanied me to the Brownies. They were big and I was still small and I felt sure they had come to protect me and keep me company. When the meeting was over, they never followed me all the way home, which I thought was good manners on their part.

I told the girls in the troop about my companions one day and the mother who was our leader looked quite alarmed. "Aren't you afraid, dear?" she asked and I assured her that the dogs were my friends.

That night, her husband walked home with me and had a long chat with my mother. Soon thereafter, I stopped going to Brownies, which wasn't really a blow, but I did miss those dogs. They had proved to me that my father's cautions against approaching our own sled dogs was just a lot of hooey, as I tearfully informed him one night at the supper table, shortly before I became an ex-Brownie. My mother remained silent but I was certain that at heart she agreed with me. I could imagine the dogs with their wolfish smiles, happily racing beside her as she drove the groceries home on her tractor.

Chapter Twenty-one

My mother's conviction that she'd be dead by the time she was fifty, a belief buttressed by a family history of faulty hearts and her own frequents bouts of high blood pressure, was ameliorated by another strongly held belief. She knew that when she turned forty, she would begin to reclaim her own life, an existence that would be separate from the demands of a household and children.

She had to tailor this ambition to those who were making the demands upon her. My father's vision was now so impaired that he could no longer work and our family was supported by disability payments from Social Security. Her youngest child was seven. Not being the sort of woman who would abandon a blind husband and five children, my mother began to plan. We would, she decided, all run away from home together.

She'd been practicing the art of escape for the past year, which was made possible by a decision she had made for me. When I was ready to go to high school, she had looked at the educational options available in our area, decided they were below her standards, and had ordered a 9th grade correspondence course. She had seen how smart girls in our part of the world turned into small-town femme fatales as soon as they left elementary school; high school was the rural Alaskan equivalent to a coming-out cotillion that lasted four years. It was considered normal to pick up a diploma and a marriage license almost simultaneously. Although I was far from femme fatale material, my mother decided to play it safe. I stayed home.

Part Two
What She Gave

My father was at that time still able to work for wages, in the oilfields that were a substantial distance from our homestead. He came home only on weekends, with my mother driving up to get him on Friday and taking him back on Sunday, not returning to us until Monday. While she was away, I at fourteen filled in for her as the head of the household.

The carrot for me was that somehow, someday, my parents would find a way to send me to New York, where I would go to Cathedral High School, the all-girl Catholic school that had educated my mother. For the three days a week that my mother slipped the bonds of domesticity and I prepared meals and made sure small children went to bed on time, she and I both plotted our future lives.

While I imagined the joys of walking on concrete sidewalks rather than lanes of mud, my mother dreamed of the call of the open road, smooth ribbons of asphalt leading her to places she had never been before. Neither of us was too keen on the grim details of reality. For us, it was the big picture that mattered. Silently and privately we constructed our new existences, with the certitude that if we wanted them enough, they would come true.

There's a peculiar fate that befalls Alaskans who isolate themselves. They become "bushy." It's a state characterized by an inability to conform to social manners. Small talk is the first to go, followed swiftly by a form of extreme agoraphobia. Being with more than four people in a room holds agony for someone who's gone bushy, and being alone is the highest form of contentment. While my mother was blossoming under her newly found freedom of outsourcing her household responsibilities to me, I was closing up, changing from a wildly sociable little girl to a painfully self-conscious adolescent. The only rules I observed were those demanded by my precocious role of domesticity.

It was absolutely the wrong time to have sealed me off from the world, but none of us knew that—not yet. The idea that it might prove difficult for me to move from an Alaskan homestead to midtown Manhattan never occurred to my parents. For me, a girl who still believed in magical transformations, I was sure that a new existence would provide a whole new me, a self that was lying dormant until the right time. Of course Mowgli the Wolf Girl could become Holly Golightly; it would happen in the following chapter. It always did in the books that had become my only link to an outside world.

Meanwhile my mother spent her solitary time behind a steering wheel, mulling over her means of escape. When my father could no longer work and we all simmered together in our house on the hill, it became apparent to her that leaving home was the only rational choice. By this time, we were all expert at leaving and taking up a temporary residence somewhere else, but my mother's ambitions went far beyond that. It soon became obvious that my yearning to be a gypsy was hereditary.

It was traditional in our family that after breakfast on cold and cloudy mornings, my parents sat near the fire, drank unlimited cups of coffee, and talked. Now they had mornings stretching before them into infinity, with nothing more pressing than making sure there was enough firewood, and this alarmed them both. My mother presented her idea and my father kindled to it.

They announced it at supper one night, taking us all by surprise. "How would you like to go on a camping trip next summer?" my father asked.

Our family trips had been limited, but I remembered the time when we had camped across the United States and Canada, after our winter in Manhattan. I put down my fork and sat up a bit straighter. This could turn into a discussion with possibilities.

"Your mother," he continued, "wants to camp across Canada to Newfoundland, drive down to visit your relatives, and then—who knows? She thinks Mexico is a good idea."

"We'll sleep outside every night," my mother said happily, "and each meal will be a picnic, always in a different place."

"But what about Princey?" my smallest sister asked, looking worried. Prince was her dog, by his choice, who spent his life trying to herd her into positions of safety.

"We'll find people who will take care of the animals," my father said briskly, knowing this was a point upon which active dissension might rest, "They can't go with us, but they'll be happy to see us when we come back."

This was a bold-faced lie. Prince made his way back to the family he loved twice after being taken to a neighbor who lived twenty miles away and the cats all ran off into the woods after they were taken to their new homes. But at the time, none of us knew that was going to happen, perhaps not even my father. He beamed at us, disaster averted.

My mother was radiant. While my father explained his design for a grub box, which would hold all of the utensils and basic food stuffs needed for our meals, "our little kitchen," my mother described the joys of being able to stop whenever we wanted, and the thrill of sleeping near the Atlantic Ocean, listening to the sound of waves in the darkness.

We had all winter to plan our journey. I began to pore over back issues of the *National Geographic* as if they were mail-order catalogs. Canada and Mexico were generously represented in glowing photographs and flattering words; Taxco and Prince Edward Island were the destinations I lobbied for most heavily at the supper table.

"You'll see Prince Edward Island maybe, but you'll never make it as far as Mexico," my father announced, "We're dropping you off in New York City, kid. You're going to stay with your grandmother and go to Cathedral, the way we always planned."

I looked at my mother, who was nodding happily at the other end of the table. Mexico began to fade back into the piles of yellow and white magazines, replaced by postcard images of Fifth Avenue and advertisements from the *New Yorker*. My mother's daughter to the core, I refused to let memories of my grandmother's shoebox apartment, its entryway holding a Pullman kitchen, its scrap of a living room dominated by a small nonworking, marble fireplace, and its postage stamp bedroom just big enough for a single bed and a nightstand, intrude upon my Manhattan fantasies. Besides, I would have argued had anyone brought up questions of space, I'd be in school all day and then I'd be outdoors, exploring.

My grandmother, since I had last seen her when I was six, had become a page of cramped penmanship that arrived in an airmail envelope five or six times a year, and a roll of comics from the Sunday papers that she encased in a brown wrapper and mailed to us. My mother rarely talked about her; they never corresponded. I had no idea of who this woman was, but she was indubitably a grandmother and in fiction they were loving, generous women who adored their grandchildren. My grandmother frequently observed in her letters that I looked just like her. She would dote upon me and for once in my life I would be the cherished only child, finally escaping the frequently voiced truth, "You're the oldest. You're responsible."

My grandmother was old, at least sixty. I could be helpful to her, as she hobbled into her dotage. These were all unshakable convictions as I imagined my future life, and nobody bothered to provide any other details. Although I energetically wrote to provinces and states all winter, sending away for tourist brochures, my attention was claimed by the streets of New York and the gift of being there on my own.

My sisters and my little brother had, over the past years, become chores. There had been far too many days when I was chained to the house because of them, preparing their meals and cleaning up afterward, making sure they washed their hands before eating. Somewhere along the way I had stopped realizing how much I loved them, although my brother and baby sister were quite demonstrative in showing how much they cared for me. My ration of hugs and kisses from them was generous and having a small hand slipped into mine when I went outdoors was a matter of routine. Never once did I imagine how it would be to live without them.

I had fought so fiercely to be an individual that my place in our family and the support I derived from that no longer was something I gave thought to. I turned fifteen with the comforting knowledge that within the year I'd reclaim my birthright, my place in one of the world's great cities.

Immersed in their own dreams, their own plans, my parents had no time to

wonder about mine. We moved through that winter in happy, private fogs
of fantasy; if anybody else in our family didn't think that this was their idea
of high adventure, they kept those thoughts to themselves.

I should have remembered the day, twelve years earlier, when my father
took us in the jeep for a drive on the beach.

Beach cabin near Cook Inlet

Chapter Twenty-two

Back in the days when I was so little that I had only one baby sister and our family could still fit in a small army surplus jeep, all of us set off for Cook Inlet. It was rare that my mother was involved in one of these expeditions and there was a festive feeling to the outing, even though the trip was probably quite mundane. As well as providing an unlimited supply of clams for anyone with a shovel and a tide table, the beach also yielded soft, brownish-black coal that burned too quickly and left too much ash, but it was easier and more fun to gather than firewood.

It was too cloudy and windy for the baby to spend much time outdoors, but rather than forgo the pleasure of our excursion, my father suggested that we drive along the beach for a while and see what we might find.

At first the sand was as smooth to drive on as a paved highway. The tide was out; miles of grey satin stretched in front of us and as far as we could see to our right. On our left was a high bank with stiff, sharp spears of grey-green beach grass sprinkled with wildflowers, and trees that had been windblown into gnarled shapes. Piles of driftwood, smashed together by storms, made intriguing little houses that were just my size, and the large rocks that towered near them looked like small castles. I stared as we drove by, imagining what sort of people might live in these shelters and wondering if they ever had anything to eat other than clams.

The tire marks of vehicles occasionally formed driveways up from the beach, barely visible in the tall grass. The bank became higher and the tracks vanished, leaving no signs that anyone else had ever been where we were now, until we passed a cabin that was snuggled into a large number of straight and substantial spruce trees, far from any road. It had been built on the slope of a hill that was forested right up until the sand took over. There was no smoke coming from the stovepipe and no vehicle was parked nearby. "That's Joe's place," my father said, "he's back in the states right now."

I was sorry nobody was home; my legs were tired of sitting and this looked like the perfect place to play while my parents visited over a few cups of coffee. The jeep was bouncing more heavily than it had been a few minutes before; we were hitting rocks that stretched out in pancake shapes under our wheels. Some were riddled with holes and looked like grey Swiss cheese, others were folded into weird layers like pieces of fabric spun from stone. My father had to concentrate on steering through them and our journey was no longer smooth. "We could break an axle on these damned things," he muttered and my mother said very quietly, "The tide's coming in."

"There'll be another cabin along the way," my father said, searching for strips of unbroken sand. But as he drove, the hills turned into high, steep bluffs on our left. To the right an edge of waves was devouring the wide field of sand that had seemed endless an hour or two earlier.

"We're closer to Homer than we are to Anchor Point," my father said and his smile disappeared. The flat rocks gave way to a kind of rough gravel and pebbles hit the windshield as my father increased his speed. The bluffs had become cliffs. I could see cabins high above us, but there was no way to reach them. My father stopped just long enough to grab a five-gallon can of gas from the back and quickly refuel the jeep. My mother said nothing at all but she grabbed my hand and her grip was tight.

The day was fading fast and my father had to turn on the headlights. By the time that we drove away from the cliffs to a trail that took us up to the highway, it was pitch dark. We followed the road through the trees into Homer's main street, where a café was still open. I was given a bowl of ice cream and I'm sure my parents each had a very stiff drink.

Light and Silence

Not until years later did I ask my parents exactly what had gone on during that trip and why it had ended with ice cream. My father admitted he had forgotten to check the tide tables before taking his wife and children for a drive on the beach and that the jaunt could have ended very badly.

A can of frozen chainsaw gas that he brought into our warm little cabin to thaw resulted in the conflagration that had left us without a home. After his vision made him a road hazard and he was advised not to drive, he took me for a ride in our jeep one day and drove straight over the side of the highway. We plummeted down into a small ravine and I wore a sling to support my right arm for a week.

I had learned that my father's ideas always needed a bit of scrutiny, but this new plot had been hatched by my mother. That was a novelty and her track record was unblemished. It never occurred to me that a trace of my customary skepticism might not go amiss.

Cook Inlet beach rocks

Part Two
What She Gave

Storm over Kachemak Bay

Light and Silence

Chapter Twenty-three

It was almost break-up, the time of year when rivers thawed, snow melted and the world became a mass of slush and mud. The snow was soft and dirty around our house, making mobility irksome, and we stayed indoors more than we did in winter. The air was becoming warmer, the light was returning, and the evenings were long.

Good Friday was always a solemn day in our house. We had been denied countless movies, birthday parties, and invitations to spend the night because they coincided with the commemoration of Jesus's death. Being the semi-pagans that we were, to us children Good Friday meant little more than two final days of enduring whatever Lenten sacrifice we had been forced to make and only one more morning before we woke up to find Easter baskets beside our beds.

Even when life was at its most stringent, my mother was a firm believer in Easter baskets and egg hunts before breakfast. For weeks she had been dipping oval-shaped white fondant into melted chocolate to make bitter-sweet candy eggs that we were forbidden to touch until Lent had faded into Sunday morning.

We were sprawled all over our house that late afternoon, my mother in the kitchen, my father talking with a friend in the living room, the rest of us off in our bedrooms. When the house began to tremble, nobody paid attention. Small earthquakes were routine matters and we had all become thoroughly bored with them. The trembling became a jolting sort of sway, our windows

Part Two
What She Gave

began to rattle, and the visiting neighbor yelled, "I've been through these before in the Middle East—everybody get outside."

He was a taciturn man; hearing a speech of this length come out of his mouth made us all obey without argument. The staircase that led to the back door had become violently unstable, and it was difficult to keep our footing as we made our way out of the house.

Three minutes can be a very long time. All of us clung to our big, heavy station wagon as the ground beneath our feet moved back and forth rapidly, with enough force that our car rocked in that same motion. The large spruce trees behind our house were bending in the still air; the snow that had collected on their branches all winter fell to the ground in white sheets.

My mother was facing our house, positive that she was losing her mind. As she stared, she saw the logs of the bottom story rise and fall back into place. When they parted, the gap between them was wide enough that the latest batch of Siamese kittens all leaped through the opening to escape from the house.

For years she never mentioned what she knew she had hallucinated in her fear, until much later she talked with the man who had been our visitor that day. "I've never seen anything like those kittens jumping out of your house through the space between the logs," he said. My mother almost kissed him in the relief of finally knowing that what she had seen hadn't been a burst of temporary insanity.

The ground calmed into a series of long shudders, finally becoming quiet again, and my father turned on the car radio. The only transmission was a pilot requesting permission to land at the air force base in Anchorage. When we discovered the radio stations had all gone dead, everybody began to feel frightened.

The stations were back on the air within half an hour, broadcasting through the use of emergency generators. Anchorage was devastated; buildings had fallen, houses were ruined, streets were torn apart. Seward was on fire, and coastal towns were being told to evacuate because tsunamis were probably on the way. There was no news yet from the small towns and villages; that came through in a slow trickle all night long.

We pulled our mattresses down the stairs and huddled together near the stove, listening to news reports. Each time a new quake shook the house, we all rushed for the door. By the third time, my father told us to sit tight. "These are aftershocks; they'll go on all night. We can't panic. The earth's just settling back into place again."

There were eleven aftershocks that night and into the next morning. There would be almost 300 more in the following three days and thousands in the months to come. The first ones were almost as violent as the earthquake had been, although much shorter. We sat on the floor and heard our house squeal as it moved around us, but it stayed in one piece. We were lucky.

Overall, Alaska was lucky. Its population was small. There were 250,000 people living in the state in 1964, with 100,000 of them in Anchorage. Because the earthquake hit in the early evening on Good Friday, most people were at home. The schools were empty and so were most of the offices. In the entire state, 115 people died.

Their deaths were horrible. In one of Anchorage's most wealthy neighborhoods, huge cracks opened in the ground under people's feet, engulfed them, and then closed shut again. A boy I had gone to school with a year earlier was swept away with his mother in the tsunami that destroyed Valdez. An Aleut village was wiped away by the wave, along with almost half of the people who lived in it.

Seismic instruments were inaccurate in those days when an earthquake measured more than 8 on the Richter scale. At first we were told our quake had been 8.6; later that number changed to 9.2. The initial aftershocks went as high as 7.

The earthquake had lasted anywhere from three to almost five minutes, depending upon location. Its force, we were told, was more than 10 million times that of an atomic bomb. In Valdez, it had smashed a 10,000- ton cargo freighter into the dock. A 98-foot tsunami swept the vessel onto dry land and then took it back out to sea. Buildings along Fourth Avenue in Anchorage dropped eleven feet; the ground in a 30-block residential area of the affluent Turnagain neighborhood had liquefied and slid into Cook Inlet.

Undersea, the ground in some places had been lifted by as much as fifty feet, and parts of Alaska's coast had been struck repeatedly by destructive waves that raged until early morning of the next day.

The news continued to seep into circulation over the following week. We saw the photographs in *Life* and *Time* magazines; much later we would spend time in the lunar landscape of Anchorage's Earthquake Park, a grey and barren mass of upheavals, folds, and craters, where the ground had been shaken into what has been called "alluvial jello," liquefied clay.

Panoramic view of Kachemak Bay mountains

Within a month we were packed into our station wagon, pulling out of our driveway, my mother behind the steering wheel. Seven of us, along with our camping supplies, made a tight fit. Every night, every morning, through Canada and the continental United States, we would unpack and then reload our tents, sleeping bags, and air mattresses.

I was dropped off in Manhattan to live with my grandmother. My family camped their way down the length of the Eastern Seaboard, as far as the Florida Keys. They flew to Puerto Rico and found a large house on the edge of a sugar cane plantation near the city of Mayaguez. It had been grand at one time, with a verandah that extended along three sides of its front, but now rats lived in its attic and ants crawled into the bowl of batter when my mother made pancakes in the morning. Instead of glass, it had wooden shutters at its window openings, and a large mango tree dropped its fruit all

Part Two
What She Gave

over the front yard. My brother and sisters went off to school once again, and my father embarked on a partnership with a local businessman to build boats from ferro-cement.

In New York I wore a school uniform, went to museums, used three different branches of the public library, wandered through the streets, made a few friends with other girls at Cathedral High School, and learned to be alone in a way I had never been before. So much of what passed as normal to the people around me was inexplicably exotic to me: the 60 degree sunlight that melted icicles on Christmas Day, the bears behind bars at the zoo who greedily ate butterscotch Lifesavers tossed into their cage by a passerby, the men who carried umbrellas to ward off a snowfall.

I began to miss the sight of stars and the feeling of solitude. At night I often climbed the service staircase of the West End Avenue apartment building where my uncle lived and where I was soon deposited by my grandmother, comforting myself with the few hazy, flickering constellations that pierced the city's radiant glow, hungry for a few minutes when I could stand completely by myself, away from crowds of strangers.

I rarely received letters or phone calls from my parents, and for the first time in my life I was special to no one. At first this hurt immeasurably, but by the time that spring arrived and I was sent an air ticket to join my family in Puerto Rico, I was encased in a thick scar tissue of indifference. I had detached myself from home during my time in New York and I never really came back.

It would be years before we returned to live in our house on the hill. A decade later, my parents would subdivide the land that we thought would always belong to our family. The barn-like dwelling that my father had built and we had loved loomed over the windblown grass, emptied of life, holding abandoned objects, haunted and broken but refusing to tumble down.

Light and Silence

Part Three
The End of the Road

Chapter Twenty-four

It was almost impossible for me to comprehend, even though I was well past the age of sixty, the truth that my mother would never come back to being who she had once been. She'd never again tear at me with the savage sarcasm that cloaked her love, never recover from being a woman confined to her bed, never stand up and walk unaided in a direction she had chosen for herself.

Walking was so integral to the life my mother wanted to have. She had grown up striding through Manhattan; much later she would claim every street in San Francisco on foot. This was the only exercise she ever took and she did it with great style, striding briskly, arms moving freely at her sides, chin up, with a joyous and eye-catching energy. "Your mother has a real nice swing to her," observed a man who had known her since he was a little boy. When I told this to my mother, I expected her to be shocked. Instead she laughed.

Her vitality was always a beacon to me, even when I most disliked her. It gave her beauty where none really existed; it flashed in her smile, glowed in her skin, sparkled in her small eyes that were usually green, sometimes grey, and once a jaundiced yellow. It crackled when she moved through our house; it made her a live wire to be handled with respect.

It gave her a mad optimism in a life that was studded with tragedy. By rights she should have become a downtrodden drudge; the cards she was handed could have been played with the mournful power of a victim. Instead she

Part Three
The End of the Road

was a star, wherever she happened to be—Manhattan, Anchor Point, San Francisco, and then finally Fairbanks. She turned heads; her opinion was valued; her companionship prized.

She loved attention, from her children, from her friends, from people who were incidental to her. She did up to the very end. In another woman's house she granted audiences from her bed, the way Marie Antoinette would have if she had escaped the guillotine to grow old.

For sixty-four years my mother and I had butted heads, fought bitterly, talked a lot, laughed once in a while, and through it all loved each other. She taught me to drink my coffee black and was disgusted when she saw me ordering a latte. She scolded me for gulping down books, although she was guilty of doing the same thing herself. Over the years our bond had been weekly talks over a telephone. I knew that without those chats, I would lose an anchor that I had always depended upon. When she could no longer talk on the phone, I missed her. I knew I would always miss her.

I sent her breezy little cards and a book or two. I thought of her and wrote about her more than I ever had before in all our years together. And every day I moved with a frozen grief, thinking of her vivid flame, slowly dimming, flickering, almost going out.

Numb and sick to my stomach, as she lost strength, I would wake up in the middle of the night, hoping she wasn't staring into the darkness too.

Light and Silence

Chapter Twenty-five

The sun rose in a corner of deep scarlet sky on the morning that my final visit to my mother ended. In the Fairbanks airport, Japanese tourists rushed to catch the color of daybreak with their expensive cameras. I stared at it wishing I could peel it away and stick it on the wall of my mother's dark little bedroom.

Her room was narrow, wide enough for her bed, a folding chair, and an end table. A chest of drawers faced her, holding her television, her CD player, a stunning bouquet of tulips that my sister brought her, and photographs of her children. Little piles of books were stacked on the moving shelf that was attached to her bed, with more on a table nearby. A colorful reproduction of an Impressionist painting that had once hung in her homestead house was with her now, brightening one of the walls. The only window was curtained to keep out the sub-zero cold of an interior Alaska winter. This was where my mother lived at the end.

If she could have walked, she could have risen from her bed and sat in a living room that was banked with windows. Moose frequently came out of the trees to the deck and licked away the salt that had been sprinkled on it to thaw the ice. She could have played with the small dog who presided over house, and talked to his owner, Marion, a woman of style and opinions. In a room nearby was a woman in her nineties who had lived in Fairbanks all of her life. She and my mother would probably have found they had much in common, but they were two of a kind, proud and private women. For each of them, their rooms were their bastions of privacy.

Part Three
The End of the Road

My mother had become tiny. Her shoulders, which had always been broad and strong, were little wings under her flannel nightgown and her arms had only enough flesh to cover the bones. Her collarbones protruded like small jewels and the legs she had always been so proud of had turned to sticks. Her face was distilled to its essence—dominated by her eyes and her smile.

My mother ended her life not as she'd always planned, in her own dwelling place, able to take care of herself. But in some ways that was very fortunate for her. In her own house, she was surrounded by the memories of what she had been able to do, and she hurt herself when she tried to do those things—walk to a cupboard, go to the bathroom by herself, stand at the doorway to give treats to my sister's dogs. She was a woman of tremendous will and in her own home, that will refused to be quiet.

In Marion's house, my mother was a paying guest. She received tender and intelligent care, and in return, she did nothing to transgress the boundaries of the kindness that surrounded her. In a strange place, it was easier for her to accept the limitations of her body. What amazed to me was how lovingly and gracefully she entered the close of her life.

My mother could have chosen to be bitter that only at the end did her family come to her side, that during the years when she was still healthy, we all stayed away except for my youngest sister. Instead she chose to radiate love toward all of her children, who stood at her bedside when she had nowhere to run from us. The strength that it took for her to embark upon visits with people who had missed all of the stages that had brought her to this bed, the energy that it took for her to gleam her love toward us, the humor that glinted frequently as she talked, all of these things were the gifts she gave to her daughters.

The largest gift was the example she offered of how to end a good, although often difficult, life. When I said goodbye to her, we both knew it was probably forever and my mother sent me away with a smile and more love than I deserved glowing in her eyes.

Light and Silence

Cook Inlet sunset with Mount Redoubt

Part Three
The End of the Road

Flying from Anchorage to Fairbanks

Light and Silence

Chapter Twenty-six

The flight path from Anchorage to Fairbanks puts passengers on a route over mountains that jut below the plane like jagged, gleaming teeth. They stretch below for miles and I have never felt anything but comforted by them. The bones of my father's youngest brother are hidden somewhere among them. His plane was led astray by the Northern Lights and exploded in a ball of fire when it crashed into Mount Sanford. I never knew him; he was only a story that always made me feel that this mountain range is mine.

The land suddenly becomes a flat blanket, studded with lakes, broken by seams of rivers. In winter it is piercingly white and the dark ribbons of trees are soothing in that relentless light. Then in the curve of one of the rivers is an unlikely cluster of buildings that is Fairbanks, still an outpost long after its Gold Rush days.

The airport is small and the runway that the plane locks into feels like a landing strip out in the bush. When I walk outdoors, the cold air singes the hairs in my nostrils. The dry purity of it is almost like breathing bleach. Even in the soft air of twilight, when the glitter of the snow is muted into a deep blue tinge, the flat white is almost blinding. The cleanliness of it overwhelms me after twenty years of being away from winter in interior Alaska.

The snow squeaks under my feet, as if I'm walking on particles of Styrofoam. I almost bend down to make a snowball, but my gloves are fashionably fingerless and the snow is too dry to pack into a shape. It turns the fading light into something magical; even at night the snow catches moonlight, the glow from windows, the beams of headlights, and shines into the darkness.

It's below zero but I've been much colder in warmer places. This dry cold is dangerously deceptive; frostbite comes without warning. Once I didn't know my hands were frozen until I tried to open a car door and found that my fingers were wooden and useless. Unlike the damp chill of Anchorage with its knife-blade winds sweeping off the inlet, the winter cold in Fairbanks is seductive. It holds the frozen doom that Jack London wrote about in his classic short story, *To Build a Fire*. It's beautiful right up to the moment that it becomes deadly.

I once tried living alone in a little cabin with a wood stove the winter that I turned twenty. I scavenged wood from old mining sites until I'd taken all that I could carry. My last fire was built from a long, thick plank that I'd dragged home. I had no saw so it projected from the small stove onto the floor. The next morning I packed my suitcase and flew home to my parents.

Heat is almost an entity in Fairbanks and people pay dearly for it. Alaska's legendary high paychecks are devoured by winter heating bills and every place I went on my last visit was much warmer than the temperature I maintain in my small Seattle apartment. When I lived in my own Fairbanks house, I often kept the thermostat hovering around eighty. Inside nobody wants to feel the slightest hint of cold. Houses are kept at a temperature in which orchids could flourish.

Outside the large window of my sister's living room is a river that is fed by the one that flows through downtown Fairbanks and stretches toward the outlying hills. In February, in town, the smaller river is still moving, open water. In the olden days, it froze so solid that when it thawed it often took out the bridge. Even twenty years ago, people rode their snowmachines on the ice of the Chena River. Now my sister says she won't walk out on river ice anymore.

The sight of a moving river at the coldest time of the year hit me hard as we flew over the Chena before landing in Fairbanks. For an Alaskan, that's

Light and Silence

a sight as surreal and unsettling as the melted watches in Dali's *Persistence of Memory*. I push the image out of my mind with mental snapshots of stunted black spruce made lovely by the snow that covers their branches, of deep blue shadows caught in the tiny crevices of a snowbank, of all the beauty that I refused to acknowledge in the years that I struggled to leave Alaska.

The strong surge of love that I felt for winter when I made my final visit to my mother in Fairbanks surprised me, until I understood that it wasn't my own passion that held me. It was her love for Alaska that briefly and thoroughly took over my eyes and my heart, at last making me understand why she had brought me to this place, and why she always returned to it. My vision, not for the first time, had been usurped by my mother's dream.

Mountains near Fairbanks

Part Three
The End of the Road

Mount Redoubt

Light and Silence

Chapter Twenty-seven

My dreams have all grown out of the ones that were held by my mother. The passion and longing I felt for New York as I was growing up were feelings I had absorbed from her own homesickness, and I too live with the heart-tearing ambivalence that comes when a person loves two parts of the world and can only reside in one. It causes me to go to Southeast Asia and China every chance I get and that too is a legacy that came directly from my mother.

When I was seven, she gave me a copy of *Anna and the King of Siam* and that gift was as prophetic and fruitful as the present her father gave to her at the same age. Although I wasn't as haunted by Mrs. Leonowens as my mother was by *The Snow Baby*, it certainly made me eager to go to "Siam" when I was finally given the chance. My mother was sad to have me go so far away, but in more ways than one, she had planted that seed.

She was a woman who thought she was headed north but instead ended up as far west as the road would take her. Farther to the west, straight across the Bering Sea that all of Alaska's bays and inlets branch from, is Siberia and then Japan. Alaska's Aleutian Islands stretch closer to Asia than the Hawaiian islands do; Attu is closer to Hokkaido and Tokyo than it is to San Francisco and Los Angeles.

I once knew a boy from Alaska's Saint Lawrence Island, who told me the men in his family still continued to travel by boat across the 30 miles of water that separated them from their blood relatives in Siberia. Mongol

Part Three
The End of the Road

faces were the predominate ones in my Alaskan landscape after my family moved away from the white village of Anchor Point, and as a short, dark girl who grew up in the bush, I felt more at ease with Alaska's indigenous population than I often did with urban white people. When I finally went to Thailand, the faces I saw there were comfortingly familiar to me; in some ways I felt more at home in that country than I ever did in Manhattan.

Although we were told we were growing up on the Last Frontier, as coastal children, we didn't see the end of the land and the beginning of saltwater as our ultimate boundary. That was simply a launching pad for new exploration. My Maine ancestors took to the sea and sailed west to Asia by going east toward Europe, around Cape Horn, and then north to Japan and China. My own route was one that was much less convoluted. My mother placed me in the west, pointed me straight toward Asia, and obediently, I continue to travel in the direction that she gave me.

My mother as a young wife, 1947

Light and Silence

My mother didn't want a memorial service, or mourners gathered by her graveside, or a wake. Without these rituals to help defuse my grief, I chose a way to honor and remember her in a form that would have pleased her. She wanted her story to be preserved; one of my happiest moments as a writer was reading parts of this book out loud to her when she was dying, and seeing her smile as she listened. This was written for her. I wish she could have seen it in its finished form.

Memory is an unreliable tool and everybody has her own perspective on the past. To those people who may disagree with my point of view, I have four words. Write your own stories.

I have not used surnames for a reason. Those who know don't need them; neither do those who don't know. The stories are what are important and through them is the way my mother would want to be presented.

I'm indebted to Sheri Quirt, Kim Fay, Mary Mullen, and Susan Blumberg-Kason, all gifted writers and discerning editors who provided invaluable suggestions that saved me countless moments of embarrassment. And to Albert Wen, I send my deepest thanks for making *Light and Silence* become a book.

Also by Janet Brown

Almost Home
2013, ThingsAsian Press, 5 1/2 x 8 1/2 inches; paperback; 210 pages; color images
ISBN-10: 1-934159-55-7
ISBN-13: 978-1-934159-55-2
$12.95

"In *Almost Home*, Janet Brown writes with the affability of a wise local who's delighted to stroll with you through her Asian city streets and wryly point out all the things you wouldn't have noticed if you'd gone on your own. That's what travel writing is all about."—Colin Cotterill, author of *The Coroner's Lunch, Grandad There's a Head on the Beach, and The Woman Who Wouldn't Die*

"Janet's talent as a traveler is to immerse herself without reservation or motive in the experience, and her talent as a writer is to convey that experience without a filter. Not for her wieldy paragraphs expounding on the social significance of this or her own emotions regarding that. Instead, you open the page and you are, simply, wonderfully, there."—Kim Fay, author of *Map of Lost Memories*

Lost & Found Bangkok
Edited by Janet McKelpin & Janet Brown
2011, ThingsAsian Press, 7 1/8 x 9 1/2 inches; 240 pages; paperback; color
photos
ISBN-10: 1-934159-21-2
ISBN-13: 978-1-934159-21-7
$19.95

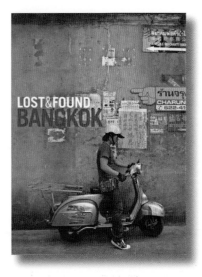

Everyone who lives in Bangkok, whether they were born there or have chosen it as their home, has a different view of the city—no two people live in the same place, even if they live on the same block.

In this book are images of five different cities through the eyes of five different residents—showing the Bangkok that they have found and hurried to preserve with a camera before it becomes lost.

Welcome to Bangkok ...explore, wander, get lost, and find your own version of this city.

Tone Deaf in Bangkok (and other places)
2009, ThingsAsian Press, 5 1/2 x 8 1/2 inches; paperback; 160 pages; color images
ISBN-10: 1-934159-12-3
ISBN-13: 978-1-934159-12-5
$12.95

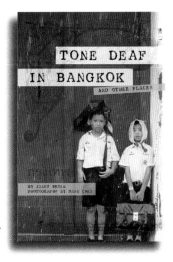

Like a Thai kickboxer, *Tone Deaf in Bang-kok* is small but packs a hidden punch. On the surface, it's the story of a middle-aged American woman who runs away from home to live in Thailand's capital city. In short, lighthearted essays, Janet humor-ously describes the hazards and pitfalls and pleasures of living the Thai life, yet her stories pose questions that lurk beneath the froth of anecdotal travel literature. Whether she's being kicked out of a neigh-borhood for behaving badly, embarking on a bitter-sweet romance with a man she knows she can never have, or discovering that there is Thai food to suit every one of her moods, she takes her readers with her and makes them feel the heat, the discom-fort and the delight of finding and settling into a new home in the world.

The Prince, The Demon King and The Monkey Warrior
Retold by Janet Brown; Illustrations by Vladimir Verano
2011, ThingsAsian Press, 8 ½ x 5 ½ inches; 96 pages; paperback; larger print; color illustrations
ISBN-10: 1-934159-30-1
ISBN-13: 978-1-934159-30-9
$9.95

Bloody battles, ferocious monsters, magical adventures and two brothers who fight against a powerful and evil king—with the help of an amazing monkey—fill the pages of this modern-day version of an epic from India.

Prince Rama, banished from the kingdom that was meant to be his, goes into wilderness exile with his wife, and his favorite brother. When the King of the Demons kidnaps Rama's wife, he and his brother join forces with Hanuman, the Monkey Warrior, to rescue her. This is the story of their struggle against man-eating giants and hordes of demon soldiers has engrossed readers all over the globe for a modern audience with dazzling illustrations and a fast-paced text, this is a book that will captivate even the most reluctant readers.

B is for Bangkok
By Janet Brown; Illustrations by Likit Q

2011, ThingsAsian Press, 6 1/2 x 10 inches; 48 pages; hardcover; color illustrations
ISBN-10: 1-934159-26-3
ISBN-13: 978-1-934159-26-2
$12.95

A day in the life of one of the world's most magical places unfolds in paintings drenched in the color and nonstop motion of Thailand's capital city. From a monk's morning blessing to the scurry of geckos at night, from splendid temples to traditional canal houses, from glittering royal barges that bring history to life to trains speeding through the sky past soaring high-rise buildings, B is for Bangkok reveals the kaleidoscopic beauty of a city that makes every day an adventure for the children who live there—or dream of living there.

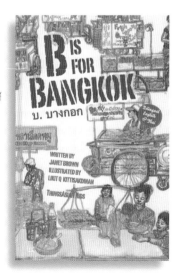

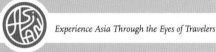